W9-BVU-434

The Languages of Theatre

Other Pergamon titles of interest

E. R. HERRMAN & E. H. SPITZ
German Women Writers of the Twentieth Century

T. H. HOWARD-HILL
Literary Concordances

R. MYERS
A Dictionary of Literature in the English Language from Chaucer to 1970

M. C. PEET & D. ROBINSON
The Critical Examination

A Pergamon journal of related interest

LANGUAGE & COMMUNICATION *
An Interdisciplinary Journal
Editor: **R. Harris**

Language & Communication is a journal founded in order to explore ways of developing an interdisciplinary science of communication, in which the analysis of spoken and written language is integrated with the analysis of other message systems involved in human and communicative behavior. The journal, which commences publication in 1981, will publish contributions from researchers in all fields relevant to the understanding of verbal and non-verbal communication.

* Free specimen copies available upon request.

The Languages of Theatre

Problems in the Translation and Transposition of Drama

Editor

ORTRUN ZUBER

PERGAMON PRESS

OXFORD · NEW YORK · TORONTO · SYDNEY · PARIS · FRANKFURT

U.K.	Pergamon Press Ltd., Headington Hill Hall, Oxford OX3 OBW, England
U.S.A.	Pergamon Press Inc., Maxwell House, Fairview Park, Elmsford, New York 10523, U.S.A.
CANADA	Pergamon of Canada, Suite 104, 150 Consumers Road, Willowdale, Ontario M2J 1P9, Canada
AUSTRALIA	Pergamon Press (Aust.) Pty. Ltd., P.O. Box 544, Potts Point, N.S.W. 2011, Australia
FRANCE	Pergamon Press SARL, 24 rue des Ecoles, 75240 Paris, Cedex 05, France
FEDERAL REPUBLIC OF GERMANY	Pergamon Press GmbH, 6242 Kronberg-Taunus, Hammerweg 6, Federal Republic of Germany

First edition 1980

British Library Cataloguing in Publication Data

The languages of theatre.
1. Drama - Translating
2. Theater
I. Zuber, Ortrun
809.2'04 PN1661 79-41711
ISBN 0-08-025246-X

In order to make this volume available as economically and as rapidly as possible the authors' typescripts have been reproduced in their original forms. This method has its typographical limitations but it is hoped that they in no way distract the reader.

Printed in Great Britain by A. Wheaton & Co. Ltd., Exeter

Contents

Contributors

May Brit Akerholt, Tutor in English, Macquarie University, Sydney. She is writing a thesis on Patrick White's drama.

Alexander Buzo, Australian playwright, has become famous for his plays: *Norm and Ahmed* (1967), *Rooted* (1968) *The Front Room Boys* (1969), *Roy Murphy Show* (1970), *Macquarie* (1971), *Tom* (1972), *Coralie Lansdowne Says No* (1974), *Martello Towers* (1976), *Makassar Reef* (1978).

Ernst O. Fink, Professor of English and American Studies, University of Hamburg, Germany. He has published several papers in the field of Theory of Translation, especially on T.S. Eliot's poetry translated into German, and the use of technical language in literature.

Reba Gostand, Lecturer in English, Department of External Studies, University of Queensland, has published several articles on Australian Drama.

Dorothy Hewett, Australian poet and playwright, her work includes poems: *Sandgropers:* A West Australian Anthology (1973,ed.),*Rapunzel in Suburbia* (1975), *Greenhouse* (1979); plays: *This Old Man Comes Rolling Home* (1967), *Mrs. Porter and the Angel* (1970), *The Chapel Perilous* (1971), *Bon-Bons and Roses for Dolly* (1972), *Catspaw* (1974, rock opera), *The Tatty Hollow Story* (1976), *Joan* (1976), *The Golden Oldies* (1977), *The Beautiful Mrs. Portland* (1977), *Pandora's Cross* (1978), *The Man from Muckinupin* (1979).

André Lefevere, Professor of Literature in English, University of Antwerp, Belgium. His books include *Classical Epigrams* (1970), *Translating Poetry* (1975), *Literary Knowledge* (1977) and *Translating Literature - the German Tradition* (1978). He translated Philippe Jacottet's *Seedtime* (1977 with Michael Hamburger), Peter Hack's *Omphale* and many others.

Franz H. Link, Professor of English, University of Freiburg, Germany. He is the author of *Die Erzählkunst Nathaniel Hawthornes* (1962), *Amerikanische Literaturgeschichtsschreibung* (1963), *Eugene O'Neill* (1967), *Amerika, Vision and Wirklichkeit* (1968 ed.), *Edgar Allan Poe* (1968), *Stilanalysen amerikanischer Erzählkunst* (1970),

Tennessee Williams (1974), *Amerikanische Lyrik* (1974, ed.), and *Dramaturgie der Zeit* (1977).

Vicki C.H. Ooi, Senior Lecturer in Drama, Department of English Studies and Comparative Literature, University of Hong Kong. Dr. Ooi published articles on Pinter and Brecht and produced many foreign plays in English and Cantonese by Pinter, Beckett, Brecht, Albee, Dürrenmatt, O'Neill etc..

Ian Reid, Professor of Literature at Deakin University, Geelong, Australia. He has published several books and articles on fiction, poetry and translation. He has also translated work by Valéry; and published a selection of his own poems, *Undercover Agent* (1978).

Marilyn Gaddis Rose, Professor and Chairman of Comparative Literature, Director of the Translation Research and Instruction Program, State University of New York at Binghamton, U.S.A.. She has written numerous works on fiction and translation and translated *Axel* (1966) by Villiers de l'Isle-Adam and *Ulyssee au Port* by Roger Ikor.

Ute Venneberg, Postgraduate student in the English Department, University of Kiel, Germany. She participated in a large-scale research project on "Modern Irish Drama on German Stages" under the auspices of Professor Buchloch, University of Kiel.

Ortrun D. Zuber, Lecturer in the Centre for the Advancement of Learning and Teaching, Griffith University, Brisbane, Australia. She is the author of *Geschichten zum Nachdenken* (1973). She wrote her Ph.D. thesis on problems in transferring American drama onto German stages (1976).

Acknowledgements

The editor wishes to express her appreciation to the Griffith University and to thank Reg Hardwick, Patsy McCarthy and Pam Christie for their advice, and Carol Owen for typing the manuscript.

Introduction

This book focuses on the various problems in the verbal and non-verbal translation and transposition of drama from one language and cultural background into another and from the text on to the stage. It covers a range of previously unpublished essays specifically written on translation problems unique to drama, by playwrights and literary translators as well as theorists, scholars and teachers of drama and translation studies. It is hoped

- that *those interested in drama/theatre* would wish to read some, if not all contributions,
- that *theatre groups* and *translators* of plays might benefit from reading about some authors' experiences in overcoming certain problems,
- that senior secondary and tertiary *students* might study the book in certain courses (e.g., English, Drama, Translation, Theatre Studies, Communication etc.) and
- that *scholars* might be stimulated to investigate similar problems in their own fields, applying the same or different methods of research.

This is the first book focusing on translation problems unique to drama. Experts in this new discipline (drama in translation studies) have collaborated from all over the world. Other recent publications on literary translation deal with linguistic problems, translation aspects common to all genres, or problems specifically related to poetry, and some of them might include the odd article on the translation of drama in particular. *The Languages of Theatre* focuses on drama translation and considers non-verbal, verbal and cultural aspects as well as staging problems, for a play is written for a performance and must be actable and speakable.

The book includes a general chapter by Gostand on the various forms, definitions, aspects and processes of the broad term "translation" (Chapter 1). Link was the first ever to have undertaken a systematisation of the interdependence of translation, adaptation and interpretation of dramatic texts in order to demonstrate the complexity of drama and theatre, and the necessity for co-operation between playwright, translator, dramatic advisor, producer and scholar (Chapter 4).

The book contains contributions by two famous living Australian dramatists on their work. Buzo writes about the translation of the written drama to the theatre performance by considering the staging of his play *Rooted* in three different countries: Australia, America and England (Chapter 2). Hewett describes how she creates and translates her ideas for a play from her imagination onto the stage and how the New Fortune, a theatre in Perth (Western Australia), influenced three of her plays (Chapter 3).

All other chapters focus on very specific aspects of drama translation which have never been dealt with or published before. The book closes with Lefevere's account of "The State of the Art" (Chapter 13) with a (minimally) annotated bibliography contained in the "Notes".

Ortrun D. Zuber
Brisbane, Australia.
October, 1979.

CHAPTER 1

Verbal and Non-Verbal Communication: Drama as Translation

REBA GOSTAND

Drama, as an art-form, is a constant process of translation: from original concept to script (when there is one), to producer/director's interpretation, to contribution by designer and actor/actress, to visual and/or aural images to audience response ... these are only the most obvious stages (no pun intended) in the process. At every stage there may be a number of subsidiary processes of translation at work.

The original concept may be an interpretation of some aspect of contemporary life, but the very act of selecting and shaping the material will inevitably translate it into something not precisely what it was before. From life it becomes theatre, theatrical, something observed as well as experienced, a product of the imagination, a creation. If there is a plot (as in Galsworthy's *Strife* or Orton's *Entertaining Mr. Sloane*), then the raw material of life has been translated into a pattern of events; if there is no plot, as in a happening (for instance, the Open Theatre's *Terminal*), there is communication of an idea, a feeling, a need, an aspiration, a fear, which may be interpreted in different ways by the participants be these actors or audience; if there is a theme (as in Sartre's *Huit Clos*, variously translated as *In Camera* or *No Exit*), then experience has been organised onto a coherent meaning, i.e. events have been translated into an intellectual pattern; if there is a didactic message (as in a mystery or a morality play, in Brechtian epic realism, or in drama for group therapy or pedagogy), then the meaning has been organised to influence thought, feeling, or action by the spectators or participants, who will translate the message according to social, political, or personal pressures within their own experience.

The medium chosen for the production, the mode and style of the production, even the physical setting (amphitheatre, circus ring, opera house, street theatre, intimate theatre, or lounge room with solitary viewer in front of the television set) and the audience for whom the production is intended - all these are inter-related aspects of the translation process, and it is not easy to speak of any one of them separately, so great is their interdependence. Within each medium, there are yet further processes of translation involved in the choice and arrangement of the verbal and non-verbal elements of theatre - the music (and all the vocal, mechanical, electrical or natural sound effects), the silences, the action, movement or immobility (including gesture, stage-business, mime, dance), the characterisation, the grouping, the costuming and make-up, the setting, props, lighting and use of colour, the use of contrast or juxtaposition, tension and pace. Every stage and feature of the dramatic production has and/or will involve processes of translation. Everything the audience sees or hears is a symbol of some reality being conveyed by the play. Symbolism, a technique usually thought of as characteristic of expressionist, surrealist, or absurdist drama, is actually basic to all drama and can be used for both verbal and non-verbal communication.

A dramatist may base the script on an established social ritual (as, for instance, in Hibberd's *Dimboola* based on the ritual of the wedding reception), or s/he may re-interpret an early myth or legend in terms of present-day life (Sartre's *The Flies* and O'Neill's *Mourning Becomes Electra* are two very different translations of the Electra story; Milgate's *A Refined Look at Existence* reworks the *Bacchae* of Euripides into the pop-culture scene). Translations of this kind may bring problems of interpretation when the audience lacks the background to appreciate the allusions or analogies; yet often there is an effective non-verbal level of emotional communication in spite of incomplete communication at the intellectual, verbalized level.

If an author chooses to translate or adapt a work from another culture, particular problems occur. Translation from one language to another will involve questions of idiom, slang, tone and style. *La dernière chemise d'amour* is not quite the same thing as *Love's Last Shift*. Irony, double entendre, word-play and puns must be communicated if the spirit of the original is not to be lost. The position that a word occupies in a sentence, for example in a language like German, may subtly influence the meaning of the original passage or may be vital to the characterization, communicating something additional to the mere surface meaning of the word by itself. Terms of endearment or of abuse in one language may provoke an inappropriate audience response when rendered too literally in another language, destroying the emotional tone of the scene. Topical allusions require careful treatment - if allusions more appropriate to the new audience are substituted, they may be out of character for the work itself, its original setting, period, or tone. If the play is in verse, should a translator attempt to produce the same rhythmic and rhyming patterns? Should s/he concentrate on the meaning, perhaps substituting blank verse, free verse, or a rhythmic prose for tighter verse patterns? A play like T.S. Eliot's *Murder in the Cathedral,* which uses a variety of verse and prose forms for characterisation and for tonal manipulation, is a challenge to the translator.

Customs, assumptions, and attitudes differ widely from one culture to another. Years ago I read an hilarious account of an anthropologist's attempt to explain Hamlet's dilemma to members of an island race whose culture made it obligatory for a widow to marry her dead hustand's brother - they simply could not understand what all the fuss was about! Eric Bentley, writing in 1949, spoke of the problems facing the Broadway producer of that period mounting a production of *The Madwoman of Chaillot:*

> *The difficulty is not only that so much of the dialogue is untranslatably French, and that so much of a Giraudoux play is dialogue. It is also that Giraudoux's plays involve so many French things and French attitudes to them. Think of the gendarmes in* Madwoman *and compare them with New York cops. Stance, gait, personality, speech, behaviour are all different ...1*

Writing more recently, Kershaw indicates how, where social habits differ between countries, there is

> *always some danger of misrepresenting the distinctions or class pressures, or the areas of reference a play is exploring.* 2

He gives the example of the critic in France who complained that the French version of Pinter's *The Caretaker* should have shown the tramp Davies drinking red wine instead of tea, because in France "tea is a drink taken mainly by genteel old ladies". But of course the play is set in England where the common habit is for almost everyone to drink tea.

Some of the problems involved in translation from one culture to another are found again in movement from one period to another. When the original work is sufficiently far back in time and sufficiently well-known, differences in attitudes or assumptions can more readily be absorbed, or ignored, by an audience: Shakespeare in modern dress is now a familiar phenomenon on the stage. But it is often more difficult to accept the underlying assumptions of a late nineteenth or early twentieth century play when this is given a more modern setting. It is, for instance, difficult to imagine a late-1970's version of Wilde's *Lady Windermere's Fan* or Pinero's *The Second Mrs. Tanqueray:* the attitudes to women and marriage simply will not wear contemporary costumes.

The dramatic style that an author chooses imposes an interpretation on his material, as can be seen by comparing plays which treat a similar theme in different modes, for instance, realistically as against expressionistically. The theme of the struggle for identity is translated into totally different stage images in Shaw's *Pygmalion*, Miller's *Death of a Salesman*, Adamov's *Professor Taranne*, or Nowra's *Inner Voices*. Similarly, the genre the author chooses imposes a translation on the material of the play: s/he may see life as a tragedy, comedy, satire, farce, romance, allegory or morality, fantasy ... A woman's frustration or passion has been viewed quite differently by Racine, Ibsen, Feydeau, Albee, De Groen.

Authors have translated earlier playtexts into a completely different kind of theatrical experience: Shakespeare has provided material for twentieth century musicals (*The Boys from Syracuse, Kiss Me Kate*) and ballet (*Hamlet*). The latter makes use of a particularly effective non-verbal image by dressing the ballerinas dancing Gertrude and Ophelia in costumes of similar cut and colour, so that to Hamlet and to the audience there is a clear equation between the two women, a similarity which the patterning of the ballet's choreography reinforces.

One phenomenon of contemporary theatre is the rise of rock-opera. Shakespeare's plays, like biblical stories, in the past provided source material for conventional opera (*Otello, Falstaff*); today Bard and Bible seem equally popular sources of rock-opera, with *Rock-Macbeths* proliferating almost as rapidly as Ionesco's chairs. Here a double process of translation is often at work: the movement is from one type of theatrical experience to another, and sometimes from one type of participant and of audience to another. Different frames of reference, even a different language, may well apply. An example of this is the "Rock Theatre" performance of *Stella* at Ipswich earlier this year (1977). The libretto for *Stella* was developed from the ideas of the Ipswich Young Theatricals and was written by Margaret Shapcott. Devised by young people for a youthful audience, the script re-sets the story of Sleeping Beauty in the "now" scene of drugs and the communication gap between parents and child, with the dialogue reflecting the in-phrases and jargon of the day: "Who flogged my sandal?" Don't get your knickers in a knot!" "I wanna blow my mind."

Adapting a script for a different medium is a translation of some magnitude, one that involves the use of differing proportions of verbal and non-verbal elements of communication. A script for the stage has been arranged for a medium that utilizes visual and aural images but is restricted to a fairly limited space, and the shape and type of stage, the facilities for lighting and for scene changes, the use of the auditorium itself by actors for entrances, exits, or even for part of the action, will all contribute something to the kind of experience being communicated. If the same play is produced on radio, communication must be entirely through the ear. Any visual elements of the original stage script that are essential to plot, characterization, creation of atmosphere or period, or to the presentation of the theme, must be translated into aural elements, for example by changing the dialogue to incorporate extra information, by introducing a narrator, or by devising appropriate sound effects. During workshops for students of drama I have found that one of the most stimulating activities is the adaptation for radio of a short stage play that contains a central mimed sequence of the utmost importance to the theme: it involves a ritual dance with a mother and father miming the struggle for possession of a child. Every group of students tackling the problem of communicating this purely visual episode in aural terms produces a different solution for it.

While radio necessarily limits the kind of images that can be communicated, it nevertheless sets the imagination free in other directions: radio is not restricted in its use of space or time. The action of a radio play has the utmost freedom to cross continents, explore outer space, probe in imagination the life after death, leap centuries or aeons; or again it can be concentrated into an intimate examination of mental processes, communicating interior monologue or mental, emotional, or physical stress. Richard Hughes' *Danger*, one of the first radio plays commissioned by the B.B.C. in 1924, used the sound of a dying miner's laboured breathing, increasing the pathos of the dramatic situation by stopping this sound just before the rescue team managed to break through. The sudden silence was like a physical blow. Writers working specifically in this medium, like Beckett, Stoppard, or Free, effectively exploit the resources of verbal and non-verbal communication it offers. The development of electronic music has increased the scope of sound effects considerably. An Australian play that makes full use of the radio medium is Marshall's *The Twinkling Ornaments of the Night*, which moves in space from Mission Control to space ship in flight, and in time from past memories to present turmoil inside the mind of the astronaut who has lost his hold on reality.

In its potential for the communication of mental or emotional states radio is rivalled by television and film, which can combine visual images with the aural images possible to radio for even more subtle "interiorization". In addition, the emphasis on visual communication peculiar to film and television can be intensified by camera and cutting techniques to give new significance to what is seen: symbols can be stressed, patterns can be underlined by montage effects to bring out relationships, or to juxtapose characters, scenes, or events in order to manipulate audience response or communicate different facets of experience. Camera angles can impose a new meaning on an apparently ordinary situation - I recall one "who-dun-it" in which the coffee-cup containing the poison loomed in the foreground of the screen, while the wife for whom it was intended sat half-crouched like a nervous cat in a large armchair in the background. Early cinema even experimented with "smellies" and "feelies" - odours released at appropriate moments to suggest the countryside in spring, etc., and electrical equipment connected to armrests of chairs in the auditorium to stimulate a tingle of excitement or fear.

Although film and television lack the spatial fluidity of radio, cutting from one set to another, exterior filming, inserted film clips and so on - some of which techniques have also been adapted for stage productions since the earliest days of cinema - can enlarge the space in which the filmed or televised play is presented. It is not dffficult to imagine the increase in emotional effect that would be possible in a filmed version of Lorca's *Blood Wedding*, using exterior scenes for Leonardo's abduction of the bride, the chase, and night and death in the forest. In contrast, the small screen of the "box" is ideal to convey claustrophobic effects, tensions and pressures. An early Australian television play set in an office used close-up shots and the confined space to image the irritations, indeed almost incestuous closeness, of a group of people unable to get away from each other, constantly rubbing shoulders in narrow hallways and crampted desk-spaces, captives of the rat-race in their little "cage".

An author, as we have seen, makes a translation from the raw material of life when choosing the mode in which the original script is written - the producer/director may well re-interpret the whole work afresh. A play written in the realistic/naturalistic style will take on a new meaning if it is treated expressionistically or surrealistically. To express aspects of Hamlet's character and to align the minor characters into significant relationships, interesting use of mirrors and masks was made in a television version of *Hamlet* a few years ago. I have seen Beckett's *Waiting for Godot* played as a tragic comment on frustration and inaction, and in another production played as broad farce. Imagine what Monty Python could do with Ibsen's *A Doll's House* or *Ghosts!* Two of Meyerhold's productions of *Harlequin, the Marriage Broker* illustrate the different ways in which a producer/ director might interpret the same script: the first, in 1911, represented

> *with its approximation of the original* commedia (dell'arte) *style a return to the naive playfullness of the tradition. Another ... had its actors, dressed in modern evening clothes, don masks representing single attributes of character; the evening dress suggested the sophistication, the masks the ambiguity of modern life.* 3

The kind and degree of training, and the sophistication, an actor brings to his art are further filters of the script performed. Actors trained for the stage, especially the conventional stages of the turn of the century, had to re-learn their art with the advent of film-making. The camera can pick up the twitch of a facial muscle, allowing for subtleties of expression not possible in a large proscenium-style theatre.

Subtle use of colours in sets and costumes, of music as a fourth dimensional (often satiric) comment on the action, and of lighting, are significant tools in the hands of the dramatist, producer/director, and the designer, influencing the atmosphere and mood of the production. Buzo's *Rooted* opens with a set in which the livingroom furniture is white, with two blue armchairs. As the action proceeds, the wife Sandy introduces ominous changes into the colour scheme - a red abstract painting, a black cocktail frock - which presage the changes she is planning in her husband's life.

The theorist Adolphe Appia, at the turn of the century, analyzed the four plastic elements in scenic design as perpendicular painted scenery, horizontal floor, moving actor, and the lighted space in which they are confined.[4] Simonson's account of Appia and his ideas are compulsory (and compulsive) reading for anyone interested in production and design. He indicates how for Appia light became both scene-painter and scene-builder:

> *Coloured light in itself changes the colour of pigments that reflect it, and by means of projected pictures or combinations of coloured light can create a milieu on the stage or even actual things that before the light was projected did not exist ... Appia's vision has made even the third dimension itself completely flexible on the stage. Space is no longer absolute. Distance, as far as the eye of the spectator is concerned, can be created as effectively by the different intensities of intersecting volumes of light as by actual spacing measured in feet.* 5.

Simonson describes a Theatre Guild production in New York, 1930, of *Elizabeth the Queen* in which the emotional effect of Essex's death is superbly translated into a visual image through the lighting and colour design: this summarizes very succinctly my thesis that drama is a process of translation. As Essex goes to his death at the end of the play, the light *through the slits of windows became brighter, almost red. And as Elizabeth straightened in her chair the first shaft of warm morning sunlight struck full upon her, turning her to bronze and at the same time plucking the (two royal--red) banners out of the shadow, turning them into bloody fangs that seemed to drip over the queen's head as the curtain fell.* 6

CHAPTER 2

Rooted in Different Places

ALEXANDER BUZO

I wrote *Rooted* in Sydney in 1968 and the play contains many direct and subconscious allusions to this particular time and place. The sun and surf, the hedonism, materialism, meat-market sexuality, off-hand transactions among the intimate emotions, the zest and camaraderie, and the freewheeling approach to metaphysics all characterised those times. But these are only the trappings of a story about the absurdist insecurity of one man.

In Australia, where journalism, sociology and literal-mindedness hold sway over imagery in the assessing of drama, the trappings of the play have been disproportionately recognised. In productions in other countries, where the trappings are either meaningless or quaint, the core of the play has been more often appreciated. There are, of course, Australians whose feelings run further than sociology, and these people understood *Rooted* perhaps better than anyone.

The three Sydney productions of the play, at the Jane Street Theatre in 1969 (directed by Rick Billinghurst), the Ensemble in 1970 (Max Phipps) and the Nimrod in 1972 (Ken Horler) all concentrated on the youthful, hedonistic exuberance of the characters. Every member of the cast was young and good-looking. The sets were white and brassy. There was a lot of physicalisation in the acting.

In the case of the Ensemble production, all the men were well over six feet tall (Serge Lazareff, Peter Whittle and Rod Williams) and the girls lissomed out at five feet ten (Lyndal Moor and Julie Chenery). The idea was that if this master race was scared of Simmo, how awesome must Simmo be? This idea is based on the old Australian joke where Big Red is rumoured to be coming to town. Everyone bolts doors as a seven foot muscle-bound giant rides in and orders a drink from a quaking bartender. "You blokes had better watch out", he says, "I hear Big Red's headed this way".

The audience reaction to these three productions was excellent. The only problem was that most people concentrated on the surface rendering of Sydney life in the 1960s and were so enchanted by this recognition that they mostly ignored Bentley and his fate. This is the luck of the game for a playwright; you can't dictate how an audience will react, and I was happy that at least their attention was held, albeit mostly on one level. I suppose that if Sydney is represented as a glittering superficial summer city, the reaction of its inhabitants must be along those lines, otherwise the vision is false. The Nimrod production, four years after the play was written, with the benefit of hindsight and maturity, was able to break through this surface to some extent.

In America it was different. Given the absurdist style of the play and the absence of normal naturalistic detail, it was possible to cast the play on an older age level. Not a word was changed in this American premiere production by the Hartford Stage Company in 1972, but all the actors were close to forty. At the time, before the beginning of the recession in 1973, many Australians reached affluence at a relatively young age and immediately responded to their national instinct to "have a place of your own". Thus Bentley and Sandy have their own home unit and have been married for three and a half years by the time they are in their mid twenties. Americans tend to do this later in life.

A popular character type in American theatre and cinema at the time was the schlemiel, a fumbling inadequate urban man possessing what was known as "hang-dog charm". Dustin Hoffman, Richard Benjamin and Woody Allen were leading schlemiels. I had supposed that Bentley would be played as a schlemiel, but director Paul Weidner cast Jack Murdock, an actor of enormous sincerity, in the role of Bentley. Kalem in *Time* magazine said of this performance:

> *As for Murdock's Bentley, it is a masterly portrait, initially of a puppy dog, later of a crushed fellow human whom no one could fail to cherish.* 1

Without playing directly for sympathy, Jack Murdock extracted the maximum in pathos from Bentley, and the audience responded to the character as a compendium of values which had to be discarded in the national pursuit of power, wealth and status. Bentley excited their sympathy and seemed to become their conscience. The swashbuckling hedonism of the Sydney productions was missing, but the gains were thoughtful and pointed.

There were few difficulties in audience comprehension of *Rooted* on other levels, either. The territorial struggle in the play is so clear, visually and physically, as Bentley is forced out of his bedroom by Sandy and out of his home by Simmo that the use of Australian slang in the dialogue did not really matter. Some members of the company and crew said they had some problems when reading the play, but as soon as they started moving it in rehearsal these problems vanished. What could be less equivocal than Sandy's handing suitcases to Bentley and saying "I want you to move out"?

A glossary was included in the programme but this was mainly a source of amusement to the audience in the foyer at interval. Certainly it was strange to hear the infallible laugh line "Yes, I've always been lucky. I won a chook at the pub once." received with silence, but this was a minor effect. As Elliot Norton said in the *Boston Record American:*

> *To appreciate it fully would probably require an elaborate glossary of Aussie slang, which seems to be more picturesque than Cockney English. To enjoy it in its American premier by the Hartford Stage Company, the playgoer needs no more than a liberated sense of humour and a passionate devotion to all those men of good will and bad luck who are habitually rooted, or uprooted, or booted by the frauds, the phonies, the predators and the perennial winners.* 2

Certain styles of writing which are geared to images, particularly black comedy, absurdism and surrealism, are easily understood in different cultures. *Rooted,* being written in this style, made contact without the particular setting getting in the way. The following quotes show how this style was detected:

> *It is Bentley's openness opposed to the apparent deviousness and malicious confidence of everyone else that creates the play's tension, and though this too is a device that Pinter invented, Buzo uses it well and understands the post-absurdist surrealism of the style.* 3

> *An invisible monster prowls through* Rooted, *an Australian breakthrough into absurdist drama being given first American showing by the very capable Hartford Stage Company. But what you don't see certainly demolishes the un-hero of this hilariously topsy-turvy suburban parable written by 27 year old Alexander Buzo. With implacable precision, wife, home, possessions and job are devoured by the absentee ogre. What Buzo is doing - like Ionesco, Beckett, Pinter - is challenging the spectator with a seemingly ultra-realistic situation that seethes with subliminal provocations.* 4

> *Rarely has black comedy been more lavish in its laughter.* 5

The London production of *Rooted* was less successful (Hampstead Theatre Club, 1973). An excellent director of ideological drama, Pam Brighton, put *Rooted* through the radical wringer and came up with five unsympathetic characterisations. Four were castigated for bourgeois materialism and Bentley was skewered for male chauvinism ("nude birds running round the terrace"). It was an intelligent and consistent production that simply played down the wrong line. The play still survived intact, but without much sympathy for Bentley, it did not provide a very nourishing evening. The fact that Bentley managed to attract *some* sympathy against such odds is a tribute to his resilience.

The director cast only English actors in this production, despite the presence in London of a foreign legion of Australian actors. She saw parallels between the lives of the characters in the play and the lives of young Britons in new towns and housing estates and wanted the play to be filtered through English eyes. Not one word was changed, of course, and although there was a glossary in the programme, the language again proved no barrier.

The actors all made very good stabs at the Australian accent, and in two cases out of five came closer to the real thing than any non-Australian ever has in my experience. Even the hedonism was captured as well as any English person could possibly manage, especially in Jenny Agutter's performance as Sandy. But the problem lay in the rigid dialectics of the production, which denied the moments of humour and pathos - although not entirely, as the play is so firmly conceived along those lines that it resisted heroically. Audience laughter and empathy cut across the ideology at several key points in the manifesto.

New drama in Australia is not necessarily ideological, and the most common stance is fuzzy left liberal. But in England, new drama almost always takes the form of truncated radical satire (as in the plays of Brenton, Keeffe, McGrath and Co.), which is occasionally well done (usually by Pam Brighton). Marxism, feminism, and humourlessness are the dominant features of this kind of theatre, which turns its back on tradition, finesse, professionalism, elocution, entertainment, style, characterisation, big central acting parts, poetry, emotion, discipline, care - everything the Australian theatre intermittently aspires towards.

CHAPTER 3

On the Open Stage

DOROTHY HEWETT

For nine or ten years I was privileged to spend the major part of my time gazing down from my study window on a replica of an Elizabethan theatre, a great open platform or forum, 43 feet by 24 feet, achieved by an architectural accident.

It was named the New Fortune after its great Elizabethan forerunner, and built to instructions by carpenters (who were rather bemused by the whole experience) in a well between three-storey tiers in the Arts Building of the University of Western Australia. These tiers are wrapped around the stage with seating on three sides. The back wall consists of two walkways between the two wings of the building with a spiral staircase running up behind the whole edifice, two balconies, and a pit for the groundlings, seated as befits a "modern" audience.

The effect of that theatre on all my future work for the stage has been immeasurable. I am haunted by its size, its atmosphere, its flexibility, its infinite variety, so that whenever I sit down to design another landscape in my head, it is always there, posing questions, creating problems and forcing me to find solutions. Even when I write a spectacle containing a Busby Berkley staircase I find I am still using the techniques I discovered on that tabula rasa. If I was asked to name the greatest influence on myself as a playwright I would say it has been the design of the New Fortune Theatre.

I have written three plays which were influenced by the New Fortune: *The Chapel Perilous* (1971), *Catspaw* (1974), *Joan* (1976). I am now working on a mock-opera, *Zimmer*, which requires similar staging.

The Chapel Perilous broke the barrier for me between the old naturalistic proscenium arch techniques, which I had been trying to transcend since about 1965, and the open stage. Even an experiment in theatre-in-the-round in a second play, *Mrs. Porter and the Angel* (1970), did not emancipate me entirely.

For a long time I had been struggling with the idea of a modern epic play set in Australia that would tell the story of a woman from girlhood to old age, struggling to become herself in a provincial landscape. As the story had to move freely in time and space and the protagonists had to live against the shifting historical and social background of their times, it created immense technical problems. I was terrified by the subject and intimidated by the problems it presented.

That same year I was teaching Shakespeare, Ben Jonson, Webster, Tourneur and Brecht, and the New Fortune was waiting outside the window of my room, with its immense size, its ceremonial quality, like an icon in the centre of the courtyard, its wrap around audience, its sense of closeness and yet alienation from the common round of human experience.

I had seen two productions there. One was a student production of *Hamlet* that somehow became unforgettable because of certain inherent qualities in the stage. I saw it on an afternoon in burning sunlight. The slow ceremonial processions along the edge of the stage, the blazing court colours, the gaudy costumes of the King and Queen, and the sombre, contrasting blackness of Hamlet seemed to burn with an intensity not possible under artificial light. When the King's crown fell from his head and rolled across the stage the sun made it glitter like the heart of kingship.

The second production was *Richard III*, directed by Dr. Phillip Parsons assisted by Aarne Neeme. This production was for me a major theatrical experience: the satanic darting figure of the hunchback, with all that immense platform to traverse and scheme upon, like a black spider weaving his web; Richard's men in their black Nazi-style uniforms; the gangster stabbing of Richard on the first balcony, leaving the body with head down, like a bleeding carcass on a hook; the pennants streamers and little flags blowing as in a football stadium; all producing a sense of incredible relevance to our own lives. After having seen this performance I knew it was possible to write and stage a modern play for the New Fortune stage that could oscillate between past and present, with the stage as a planet, the play as a parable, and only the symbolic language at its heart.

All that winter I paced the New Fortune in the rain, going back to Shakespeare, Jonson, the Jacobeans, Brecht, and finally decided that the epic theatre with its loose sequence of scenes, each one self-contained, moving like flashes across the stage, could best tell my story. The scenes could be separated by choruses, poems, songs, dances, chalked-up signs, e.g. a sign reading ETERNITY. The lonely, striving, vulnerable central figure, both heroic and foolish, could be separated off by the chorus as commentator.

But how to create a hero or heroine in such an arena? How in such a multitudinous, conflicting world as we inhabit could any hero-figure exist?

All very well for the Elizabethans with their homogeneous religious and social life, with their Chain of Being and MAN having one foot in heaven and one in hell, one part angel, one part brute. Where is *our* moral universe? Man has lost his place and his footing.

Let's look at Brecht's world haunted by beggars, ballad singers, tramps and whores, jazz and romanticism; let's look at Rimbaud, Verlaine, Genet, Lorca, Mayokovsky, the gangster movie and the western, e.g. Cagney dying in the gutter on late night telly, Edward G. Robinson's blood filling the bath, an aggressive and frivolous world, a world of squalor and savagery. This is the world of Germany 1920, the world of revolution, of economic collapse, the rise of Nazism, the America of the thirties with its murders, prohibition, crooks and adventurers, but what about Australia in 1971?

The symbolic forms of struggle used by Brecht were often boxing, wrestling and racing. Here, I decided, could be a start for such a play: the great arena of the football game, the Roman games of our civilization, a boxing ring theatre, a concrete square in a jungle of corruption. This would make the image, half-romantic, half-satirical, a metaphor for modern man and his environment, a wild, mad world with its own surreal, illogical sense, but never a trivial world. The central character must not be entirely worthless, even if a hero-villain or a bitch-heroine, he or she must have some kind of tragic lost potential. A boy on a bicycle becomes a kind of young Lochinvar; two wooden chairs and a radio broadcast make a symbolic family circle downstage left; three masked Easter Island figures have a primitive power (the lost image of an old religion); a hospital bed on rollers becomes a super-bed; an altar becomes a praying beginning and ending place or a place of judgement; a child's pram an image of our hungry frailty and tenderness; a stained glass window a burning woman.

The epic play covers a journey, an epic journey from birth to death with its roots in mediaeval theatre, each central protagonist an Everyman or Everywoman, and because the stage is THE WORLD and the journey is through time and space and there are no unities, then the stage *must* be as bare as we can make it. It must be a great bare platform created by language, movement and song, an image of the world; but what image can we project? Perhaps we can only create the ghost of a moral and ethical universe. Left alone in the great space, what world can the playwright make? A corrupt, confused, fantastic, extraordinary and lonely world. What can he do with his lonely characters? They will be a fantastic, confused, corrupt and contradictory lot, but can they be at least potentially heroic? One measures them not against a world of over-stuffed furniture with tightly closed windows, framing a snow mountain or a frozen fiord they can only yearn after, but against a world where they are riding foolishly with feathers in their hats to their doom - like the young Hedda Gabler. They have never gone INSIDE, they are on the HEATH in the storm, and ROME and TIBER melt around them. Although diminished by the modern world they will refuse to give in, they will not capitulate from that stage, no matter how puny and fragmented their quest now seems. Out there they have some inalienable humane sense of their own power to myth-make.

Since the modern world is composed of so many unreconcilable elements, the elements of such a play will seem unreconcilable, yet forced together, linked by a series of unbreakable chains; the marching feet, the chorus scenes, the blow-ups, the songs (popular, obscene, hymnal), amplified voices, film clips, and sound and light effects signifying nightmare and transfiguration.

The lonely, domestic, interpersonal relationships must be performed in a spot or on a small raised platform, downstage centre.

For productions on the open stage it is necessary to walk a tightrope between rough realism and symbolic extension, never losing touch with the realities of external life. Like all good fairy-tales such plays must be grounded in reality, there must be bridges between the plays and the lives of the audience, the commonplace idiom they speak, the stuff of their dreams, their nightmares and their secret inner lives.

The Easter Island-type statues designed for the Authority Figures always present on stage in *The Chapel Perilous* were transported into my small front garden after the first season in Perth was over. The local children going past, whispered "A witch lives there" or "I think it's a Church". That stage with its symbolic Mystery Figures so easily became the world, the school, the university campus, a 1939 suburban house, Victory Day in the streets, Hiroshima, a bedsitter, a factory, an empty beach, a court-room, and a place of judgement and death.

Against that backdrop moved the long crocodiles of schoolgirls, political, secular and religious processionals, the games of Oranges and Lemons, the sweeping on and off of the chorus playing its many faces. The extra-ordinary pace possible on the open stage helped to make the pattern of the unreconcilable reconciled. It was both a highly fakeworld and a real one and each component fed the other.

There is plenty of room to move on the open stage. It is even possible to use the power of religion still, the primitivism of the chant, the nostalgia of the hymn, the memory of belief, the last of our mass celebrations, the church, the political rally, christenings, weddings, court scenes, death-bed scenes, hospital visits, burials, Anzac days, Christmases, Easters, discos, sports arenas, pop concerts and all the rituals that still partly belong to us in our shattered society.

What language do modern characters use on such a stage? Naturalistic dialogue with a strong rhythmic sense and use of images, heightened prose, ritualistic chants, songs, sermon-like speeches, repetition, poems, the interior monologue, the aside. We can use the most brutal degradation and poetic elevation within the same sentence. But we must never for a moment let the audience forget that they are in the theatre. One of the bonuses of the open stage is the strange closeness and the instant, where rhetoric and a whisper co-exist.

There is a vast loneliness out there, because, in a sense, we have never escaped from the foggy Danish walls of Elsinore, or the storm-ridden heath. On such a stage it is possible to tell a story that is a chronicle of the times, a moral fable. We can be anywhere and everywhere within a moment, but always we are IN THE THEATRE, sharing together a ritualistic experience of great size, not looking through a keyhole into a box with four tight walls.

How does such a theatre create a communal feeling? Is there some spirit of reconciliation abroad in such a place? I believe there is. It is perhaps created by the sheer size, the circular movement of the processions, the relationship to the elements. This stage does not whirl the actor into a central vortex that seems to minimize him (e.g. The Tyrone Guthrie Theatre in Minneapolis). The actors must be in control of *all* the space and use it; this gives them a most extraordinary free-flowing, kinetic sense, not just physically, but spiritually. One cannot be puny on such a stage, one must have some kind of stature, and the actor clad in his own essential humanness is not to be sneezed at. Therefore, this great stage dictates a certain tone and style which cannot, in the long run, minimize the human creature.

The central protagonist of *The Chapel Perilous* is Sally Banner, the minor provincial poet and long-haired rebel. This difficult role was created by the actress Helen Neeme in the first production at the New Fortune. Helen Neeme, a "vulnerable" actress, projected an extraordinary mixture of extrovert/introvert qualities on stage. I will never forget her standing in a gentle rain (the New Fortune stage is open to the weather) speaking the opening lines borrowed quite shamelessly from *Morte d'Arthur* with a dash of *The Waste Land*, playing a flawed female Lancelot setting forth on her perilous and "failable" secular journey. In her school uniform with the rain falling on her upturned face she was elevated and illuminated because of her relationship with the elements, because of her language, and her placing on that empty platform. Perhaps this sounds too far fetched: a black-stockinged schoolgirl and the Holy Grail. One wonders how it can work for us still, but it does.

It works in the same way as Bob Dylan's concert at the Sydney Showground. A small, white, shining, knight-errant figure and a black-clad band of folk heroes recognized by all the Dylan buffs, the great sky overhead, a hint of rain, the groundlings seated in the thick mud, the city skyline, the words of the songs known, loved, recognized, the attitude of celebration, even prayer, as the great roar rose at the end, - all these are components of popular open stage theatre.

Why does epic theatre suit the open stage? Epic is a term from Aristotle meaning a narrative not tied to time, but transcending time, a sequence of incidents or events narrated without artificial restrictions as to time and place. This stage, then, can represent anything we wish it to be: Rome, Egypt, the Forest or Arden, Prospero's island, Mother Courage's war, with the ghost in the cellarage clanking under the trap doors. Props are few by necessity and seem to gather to themselves an extra symbolic quality because of this. There is no waste of props. Scene changes are paced out from one side of the stage to the other or upstage to downstage. Journeys, long or short, tend to be circular and/or in procession. The journey of the drop-out Cat in the folk opera *Catspaw*, from the town of Opal along the Ninety Mile Beach back to the caryard in the city called Wreckers' Yard, is a circular journey with stops for adventure along the way.

Simplicity of staging is the rule. Props must be easily transportable. Costumes can be brilliant and fantastic to draw the eye in such a vast arena. In this empty landscape actions tend to become symbolic, language tends to become metaphorical, and the whole world of the play seems charged with a mysterious force. Part of it is the challenge of a large and apparently simple place. But how complex it really is on an open stage? What characters, what language, what story will not seem diminished or out of place? How will sound reverberate there? There is no place to hide, no place to cover up inadequacies. It is like the Yorkshire moors of the Brontes, naked and passionate, demanding POWER. Nothing else will do. All tales of mystery and imagination can be told there. The stage acts as a kind of rough altar where ritual acts are performed. But as well it retains some of the rough qualities of its beginnings, the realism and earthiness of the inn yard.

The open stage helps to cure that fatal disease of the Australian imagination, the bondage to the pragmatic, to the possible, to the "real". For what is "real" on a stage? The signposts point anywhere, the landscape changes as we blink an eyelid.

In *The Chapel Perilous* Sally Banner's journey ends in death. As she returns to the school chapel to receive her OBE she also returns to the Chapel of the Self, and her life begins to make some sort of flawed meaning at last. The common life is transcended but still remains the common life. Cat, who left Wreckers' Yard for his morality tale journey into the desert to find himself, returns to the Yard sadder, wiser and somewhat chastened by the world.

In *Zimmer* the young prisoner Robin Zimmer goes whistling across the prison catwalk to become a poet in the outside world. He passes first the prisoners playing a ritualistic game of basketball in the yard, then the bandaged body of his friend Carol, burnt to death, swinging in the safety-net rigged to catch the suicides, and finally the singer/guitarist in his cell singing *I'm Not Sorry Now*.

In *Joan* the peasant girl Joan Lark suffers three metamorphoses on the road to Rouen, as Joan the Soldier, Joan the Witch and Joan the Saint. Her "real" life ends in the asylum destroyed by shock treatment. Her fantasy life begins as Joan the Saint, the doll-like icon carried shoulder-high by priests and shimmying nuns.

It is impossible to write "ordinary" characters for such a stage. A Willy Loman dwindles to dust, a Mother Courage travels triumphantly. On the open stage, villains, bitch heroines, and picaresque characters have such a wide scope to play their parts.

Australia is rich in such characters: convicts, bushrangers, water diviners, loonies, con-men, crazy patriots, speculators, adventuresses, great liars, crims, famous madams; the place is full of them still and the open stage is like a great desert from where these flawed prophets and super-criminals can be featured. Interestingly, whether they move towards comic high fortune or tragic low fortune, on this stage, the circle of their movement is always towards some kind of reconciliation. They transcend themselves and the market place to make a statement about human responsibility. Kenneth Tynan quotes Tom Stoppard, who once ended his speech on the Santa Barbara campus with these lines from the English poet, Christopher Logue:

Appolinaire said,
Come to the edge
We might fall.
Come to the edge
It's too high ....

COME TO THE EDGE!
And they came
And he pushed them
And they flew.

Stoppard was talking about the dialogue that goes on between artist and audience. It's like Gloucester teetering blind on the cliffs of Dover.

CHAPTER 4

Translation, Adaptation and Interpretation of Dramatic Texts

FRANZ H. LINK

1. INTRODUCTION

Translation, adaptation, and interpretation of dramatic texts have been the subject of numerous studies. Their interdependence has been realized, but never been systematized. If such a systematization is attempted on the following pages, it must be kept in mind that categories have to be singled out to demonstrate their position within the structure of interdependence while in reality, because of their interdependence, they hardly appear in isolation. That is, a systematization of interdependence comes close to paradox. Nevertheless, I have undertaken it to demonstrate the complexity of drama and theatre, and the necessity for co-operation between playwright, translator, dramatic advisor, stage manager, and scholar.

1.1. Narrative and Dramatic Fiction.

Translation of narrative fiction and that of dramatic fiction have many problems in common. Their main difference is due to the different communication systems they use. In prose fiction a story is communicated by a narrator. He acts as imaginary witness of something that happened and writes it down for his reader. In dramatic fiction witness, reader and/or spectator are one and the same person. There is also in dramatic fiction mediated communication, namely that of the stage-production insofar as it communicates the text to an audience. However, that kind of communication takes place on another level. One can read the dramatic text and supply by imagination all that the production has to offer. Even as reader one is a direct witness to an action without the mediation of a narrator. While in narrative fiction the narrator supplies the background and, possibly, some kind of interpretation of the action, in dramatic fiction this is supplied either by the reader and/or by the stage production. The stage production however, though limiting the spectator's imagination, supplies the information equivalent to that of the narrator by presenting it as accessory to the action the spectator is witnessing. Because of this particular kind of communication, the relation between the language used by the characters on the stage (or even in the printed text) and that of the audience (or the reader) is different from that used by the narrator and his readers. Being present at the action as immediate witness gives the impression of participation in the same system of communication or linguistic contemporaneity.

1.2. Historicity and Actuality.

Fictitious contemporaneity can be achieved in two ways, either by presenting the text as if it were contemporary to the time of the audience or by asking the spectator to imagine himself to have travelled into another time. Accordingly the play may be produced as the playwright would have done it in his time or as he would have done it had he lived at the time of a later production. We would call the first case historicism and the second case actualization. Both ways are valid even if only for the reason that it can be presumed that the playwright would have written in and for the communication system of a later time had he lived then or that he, being no longer among the living, may be misinterpreted by translating his text into the later system. Both possibilities need interpretation. It needs interpretation of how a play was or may have been produced at the time of being written as well as of how its author could be imagined to produce it in our time. Besides these two principal approaches it is, of course, possible that the two different interpretations might be valid or that the text may even be used for purposes which differ from those intended by its author.

1.3. Text and Implied Realization.

Since part of the information the narrator supplies in prose fiction is, in the case of dramatic fiction, supposed to be communicated by the stage production, the dramatic text as such is incomplete or represents the full play only by implication. Writing for the stage, the playwright assumes that his text will be produced according to the theatre conventions of his time or to what he would like those to be. So long as he assumes that it will be produced in the tradition of the theatre of his own time it is not necessary for him to make it part of his text.

The term translation has so far been used as covering any communication between author and reader or spectator. In the following remarks it will be used for verbal communication. As far as the transposition into stage production is concerned the term adaptation will be used.

2. TRANSLATION.

If the participants in the action of a play and the audience share a common system of communication this may consist of different sub-systems. Communication is possible as gesture, as dancing, as music, or as language. If the opera is sung in a language I do not understand I may still follow the outline of the plot in the acting and in the music. A similar situation is given by the performance of Japanese Nô-plays, as the ordinary audience no longer understands the language used in the plays. For the present we will limit our focus to communication by language. The characters in the play are, if other means of communication are not supposed to supplant or to prop it, using a language that the audience understands. This does not necessarily mean that they speak the language normally used by the audience. It may mean that, performing a comedy by Plautus in the original language in our time, the actors speak Latin as long as it can be assumed that a particular audience has enough knowledge of that language to be able to follow it. This, of course, would be a rather special case and the presentation of such a play is usually determined by the purpose of language learning and not by that of primarily enjoying the play as such.

2.1. Levels of Speech.

It can be assumed that the normal way of communication in a play is that of the language used by the playwright. It is understood by all who speak his language. But there are various deviations from what may be called normal, often deviations for dramatic purposes. Even what we have so far called normal may be an artificial stage language, poetic language, or it may be a dialect or a language stylized for particular purposes.

2.1.1. Contemporary Speech. The playwright usually makes his characters speak the language of his own time and country, even if they represent either people of another time or from another language group. Communication becomes a problem as soon as the language of the text is no longer understood by the audience. To bring the original text of a medieval mystery play to the level of communication of a present-day audience it has to be translated into present-day language. The text may be only slightly changed by substituting equivalents still familiar to a present-day audience for obsolete words and phrases and by speaking it in modern pronunciation. In this case the play would retain its original flavour and the audience may imagine itself to attend a performance as it was intended by its author or authors at the time they wrote their text. The choice of the one or the other possibility of translation could depend on the interpretation of the play either as dated by the particular historical circumstances of its origin, or as a form of art still accepted by a present-day audience. The quality of not being dated by historical circumstances, might be true only of parts of the play, but what matters is, to what extent it is true of the play as a whole.

If present-day language is so far removed from that of the original text that communication is no longer possible, it becomes a matter similar to that of translation from one into another language. A special problem arises when the language of the text may by and large be still understood, but no longer be considered as contemporaneous. Shakespeare's English can, in modern pronunciation, still be understood by modern audiences though it will doubtlessly miss many details. This means that the present-day spectator is still able to participate in the communication system Shakespeare used in his time; and because he is able to do so he is reluctant to translate the dramatic text into the language of his own time to make communication possible on his own level as it is regularly done in foreign language translations. As both ways of contemporaneity are valid it does not matter as long as communication on the level of the original text is not distorted by possible misunderstanding.

2.1.2. Poetic Language. As yet communication by language has been considered only as far as understanding is concerned. However, there are various levels of language to be taken into account. The characters in the play may, for example, use verse or, more generally speaking, poetic language, some kind of non-poetic standard, or colloquial speech. Without elaborating possible differentiations further, it may be said that poetic or ritual language characterizes the reality in which the performance and audience participate as fictitious or as something outside or "beyond" every-day reality. The particular language can, in this case, be considered as accepted by them as communication in a particular kind of reality. Poetic or ritual language may change or the attitude of the audience to the kind of reality it participates in may change. If communication on the level of a later audience is intended, the language of the original text has, in this case, either to be translated into the poetic language accepted by the audience or into language used in every-day reality.

2.1.3. Non-poetic Language. To use poetic or non-poetic language on the stage is often a matter of convention which is apt to change in time. Poetic language usually does not change as fast as non-poetic language but the convention to use it at all may become obsolete. As far as non-poetic language is concerned the less it is stylized the faster it changes. The standard of a language may be defined as a kind of stylization, for it is more resistent to development than lower levels of speech. The playwright may have intended to use a non-poetic but nevertheless literary standard to avoid particularization in the colloquial style of his period or of social groups. The stage may develop its own style for that purpose as, for example, "Bühnendeutsch" (stage German), as far as pronunciation is concerned. Colloquial speech or even slang might be used to keep characters as close to reality as possible. But the closer a playwright tries to keep to reality the sooner the language drifts away from it in terms of time. This becomes quite obvious in plays of the naturalistic period or of our time. To keep the intended closeness intact, plays written in colloquial style or slang should be permanently translated to the correspondent language at the time of their performance. It is often done on stage by the actors using their own style of colloquial speech or slang.

2.1.4. Dialect. Dialect speech is apt to change as fast as lower colloquial speech or slang. Though colloquial speech may be recognized and accepted by the audience as belonging to the period when the play was written, dialect of a former period usually is considered as wrong, probably because it is hardly known by reading. Therefore, the play written in dialect needs translation into the idiom of the time of performance even more so than others.

Dialect and to a certain extent other group language, produces additional problems in drama. Although dialect may be the accepted language for the audience speaking it, yet a performance before an audience sharing the language in general but not the dialect will not be understood. As long as it is understood, it localizes the characters speaking it. If it is no longer understood language used must be neutralized or translated into another dialect.

When using dialect, the playwright's intention may not be to localize its action but to characterize the social status of its participants. To realize such an intention, the play must always be translated into the dialect which is recognized by the audience as being used by the corresponding social group in their part of the country. Modern playwrights using dialect for this purpose, such as Franz Xaver Kroetz, expect that their plays will be translated accordingly. Local references, of course, have to be changed correspondingly. It would sound funny if someone spoke the city dialect of Frankfurt if he is known to be a native of Basel where the action is supposed to take place. All local references have to be changed accordingly, as for example in Urs Widmer's *Nepal*. It then becomes the Frankfurt "version" of the Basel origin.

All of what has been said about the language of a play as a whole is also true of parts of the play in case different levels of language are used. For example, Shakespeare and his contemporaries used poetry as well as standard and dialect prose.

Different levels of language may be used to characterize different social strata. An example, demonstrating the necessity of continual translation into present-day equivalents, is Simon Gray's comedy *Otherwise Engaged*. In this play students of sociology speak Cockney, Oxford graduates no longer use Queen's English but middle-class colloquial speech. What will it be in another twenty years? Quite obviously differentiations such as these would be difficult to translate into a foreign language.

2.1.5. Archaic Language. So far it has been presumed that the playwright uses the language of his time. However, in many cases the actors speaking the language of their time and country are expected to impersonate characters of the past and/or of another country. This can be considered as a stage convention. After a lapse of some time the language of the play may be received by the audience as archaic and therefore be considered as adequate for characters of the past. The same effect can be achieved by the playwright if he uses a highly stylized language which will be received as archaic by the audience. Examples of this are T.S. Eliot's *Murder in the Cathedral* or the historical plays by Peter Hacks. A comparable effect can be achieved by using foreign language phrases to insinuate the foreign origin of a character. It is not important that the language spoken is as close as possible to the original it is supposed to represent, but that the audience recognizes the author's intention of stylizing.

2.2. Foreign Language Translation.

All that has been said about the language of dramatic fiction can be applied to its translation into another language. The equivalent to the original text in the author's own language would be a contemporary translation. The equivalent to a modern version of an older text would either be a translation of that modern version, as for example Eva Hesse's translation of Ezra Pound's translation of Sophocles' *Women of Trachis*, or a modern translation of the original. Problems common to all translation of dramatic or non-dramatic texts into a foreign language need not concern us in this context. Particular aspects in the translation of dramatic texts into a foreign language originate in the fictional contemporaneity of the language of the audience and that of the play. As the author uses the language of his own time, so does the translator of the play into another language. This constitutes no problem particular to drama. It is different when the play is translated in a later period. The translator will use the language of his time, and his translation will be an interpretation of the play to the extent that language is determined by its particular society and time. A successful translation again may keep the stage in a period when its language is no longer that of the audiences. The classical example of such a translation is that of Shakespeare's plays by Schlegel, Tieck and Baudissin into German. Fictitious contemporaneity is established in this case on the level of German romanticism. Contemporaneity on the level of a present-day audience requires new translation into the language of its time.

Translations of dialects in dramatic fiction into dialects of a foreign language will, according to what was said about translation from one dialect into another of the same language, be possible only if there are no localizing references or if such references can be changed to such as are imaginable in the region in which the dialect is spoken.

2.3. Unidentifiable Allusions.

With the exception of the necessity to change local references in translations of dialect plays, our remarks on the language of drama were only concerned with its literal translation. But other changes of the dramatic text are necessary when it is to be realized on the stage of a later period or of another society. Principally the text is supposed to supply all the information necessary to understand the action and its motivation. With respect to the economy of any work of art this information will be limited. The author will try to avoid everything that his audience already knows; he only has to activate this knowledge by mere allusions. The author can and does rely on a certain common knowledge of his contemporary audience. Complete understanding of a play is possible only if information supplied by the text and knowledge of the audience supplement each other. Understanding and communication no longer work if the audience does not have the information the author could expect from the audience of his time and his society.

The knowledge the audience is supposed to have and on which the playwright usually relies can be of different kinds. One kind would be the common knowledge of a society, of its history, its myths, and its customs. Though this knowledge is a matter of tradition, this tradition changes. The further the audience moves away from particular events of its own history, for example, the less it is informed about the details of these events. Shakespeare could expect his audience to know many details of England's wars with France and the War of the Roses. Today's English audience may have learned its history at school, but even so, many of the details Shakespeare is alluding to in his history plays are lost on them. This would apply even more for a foreign audience, if the translation carries over the references unchanged. For the same reason, information of foreign countries, is usually much more detailed. However, for a French audience, much of the information Shakespeare provides in the Archbishop of Canterbury's exposition on French

History in *Henry V* (I, 2) would be superfluous with regard to a French audience of the same time. Usually enough information is provided to understand the action so that no change of text is necessary in matters of that category.

The situation is different when it comes to allusions to current events and references to information which only a very limited audience would possess. A famous reference of that kind is the grave-digger's request to his companion in *Hamlet:* "Go, get thee to Yaughan, and fetch me a stoup of liquor" (V, 1, 60), probably alluding to a tavern near the Globe theatre where *Hamlet* was originally produced. If the interpretation of modern scholars is correct, the allusion was a pretty good joke at the time, but it would be lost in any performance outside its original setting. A single allusion of that kind can easily be eliminated from the text for the production. It can also be easily substituted by reference to an equivalent to Yaughan's tavern near the theatre in which the play is produced. It becomes difficult to arrange an older text for a modern production if the understanding of the plot depends on the audience's knowledge of contemporary events, or if allusions of that kind constitute too large a part of the text, as is the case with most of the comedies of Aristophanes.

It is, of course, comparatively easy to supply a modern equivalent to Shakespeare's joke in his allusion to Yaughan's tavern. Part of the joke at least consists in the anachronism of bringing a tavern near the Globe into an imaginary Denmark of the eleventh century. It becomes a problem if the allusion to information accessible to the audience turns up in a serious context. In comedy, allusions to events contemporary with the production supply an additional source for laughter. A well established pattern may be seen in the songs of Nestroy's comedies on the German stage, where whole sequences of additional verses referring to events of the time of their present-day production are introduced. Their anachronism intensifies their comic effect.

As the example of Shakespeare's Yaughan shows, the common knowledge expected by the author from his audience may be that of a very small group. It may be that of the regular audience of a particular theatre, that of a town, of a country, or even of all theatre-goers of a certain period. The smaller the group implied, the more it becomes necessary to amend the text of the play if it should be produced before another group. The easiest method of emendation, of course, is cutting. To supply corresponding references is easiest in comedies or comic passages of other plays as they often are characterized by breaking the illusion of the fictional world on the stage and as their possible anachronism provides an additional comic effect. Information irrelevant to certain audiences can easily be cut. Information no longer to be expected from later audiences can be supplied by new prologues, play-bills or - and particularly on the present-day stage - by the introduction of a narrator or commentator. The prologue to Brecht's *Antigone*-version is a good example of providing additional information after the lapse of more than a thousand years between ancient Greece and present-day Germany.

Emendation of the text may become necessary not only because knowledge differs from one audience to another, but also because of varying attitudes towards the theatre as such or towards the morals prevalent on its stage. The extreme case is closing the theatre altogether as it was done by the Puritans in seventeenth century England.

Other references possibly due to change are those to the stage itself. The text may refer to stage properties not available at a later period or in the theatre of a society with a different stage tradition. As most of such references are not directly documented by the text but rather implied by the author it suffices to concentrate on their relevance for adaptation.

3. ADAPTATION.

Writing his play, the author has a particular place in mind where it could be performed, usually a building dedicated to the performance of plays, i.e. a theatre; he has a particular stage in mind on which the action could be performed, and, finally, he counts on certain traditions of performing plays on such a stage. The possibilities of realization on the stage are more or less implied in the text he writes down. Principally, the author either just relies on the possibilities available on the stage of his time, often co-operating in the transposition of the text on to the stage, or he writes down how he wants to see it realized in the form of stage directions, or he communicates his ideas by other means. It may, of course, be considered as a matter of interpretation, whether stage directions should be considered as part of the text. In the present context they are considered as not being part of the dramatic text, but as a text communicating the author's idea about realizing the dramatic text on the stage. Stage managers are less apt to change the dramatic text than what is communicated by stage directions, one of the reasons at least being that in the stage directions the author is already taking over part of the stage manager's business. Author and stage manager may be one and the same person. What matters here is the different function performed.

3.1. Theatre.

Most plays can be staged in nearly any kind of theatre. Nevertheless a performance in one kind of the theatre may be more appropriate than in another kind.

The place of performance may be determined by its relation to the every-day life of its audience. It may, for example, be a place set apart from every-day life as part of a sanctuary like the Greek theatre. The typical nineteenth century theatre was the place of a social occasion for which people dressed accordingly. The place of performance for the medieval mystery play was the market or the street: the message of Christ was supposed to be carried into every-day life. "Agitprop" finds its stage in the street as well or among working-men in a factory hall. Performance in a different place disengages the dramatic text from at least part of its intended social functions and thereby misinterprets part of its original meaning. In staging a Greek tragedy in a - perhaps renovated - ruin of a Greek theatre today, it is of course, not possible to reintroduce its former social function because the place as such no longer has it. The one effect that can be achieved in this case is that the audience may "imagine" to be in communication with the text on the level of its original setting. Staging Greek tragedy in a modern theatre requires an adaptation which will communicate the different levels of meaning the text is still able to communicate to a present-day audience. Richard Wagner's "Festspielhaus" (festival playhouse) in Bayreuth, a building constructed to provide all the mechanical apparatus and the particular acoustics necessary for the realization of his operas, set apart to provide the character of special dignity (Weihecharakter) to his productions, may be considered as a secularized nineteenth century equivalent to what was said about the function of the Greek theatre.

Besides its relation to every-day life the place of production implied in the dramatic text may reflect the social group for which it was written. Greek drama was written for the whole polis (with the deplorable exception, of course, of its women). Accordingly the theatre in which the Greek playwright could expect to see his play performed was large enough to seat all its citizens. The size of the theatre influenced not only the acting but the text itself insofar as it did not, for example, allow interiors or intimacies to such an extent as they became possible in the drama of later periods.

Elizabethan plays are well known for providing entertainment for the groundlings, the common people, as well as for the courtiers in the balconies. The construction of the public theatre of the time reflected the different elements in the play.

The classical French drama was primarily written for the court. It was produced in the court theatre. The play as well as the theatre in which it was performed were part of the life of a very exclusive society. When the middle class took over the theatre as an educational institution, it took over the topics of the play as well as the conception of the theatre as a place where they were performed, only in larger dimensions. But when its own problems became the subject matter in realistic or naturalistic drama, its theatre could no longer be considered as the adequate place of performance. New forms of the theatre as a place of staging were looked for.

These examples may suffice to demonstrate the interdependence of play, social group, and theatre. Production in a theatre for which the play was not written does not only lose its original atmosphere or ambience, it loses, at least in part, its social relevance or may distort it to an ideological superstructure distracting its audience from the problems of its own reality.

The adequacy of the theatre to the play is not only determined by social aspects. The play may consist of public or intimate action. Correspondingly, large or small theatres are adequate places of production. Beckett's *Krapp's Last Tape* can be produced in a large theatre but it would lose all its intimacy.

Another reason for choosing the place of production may be the presence of a realistic setting or a setting considered adequate to the subject of the play for different reasons. T.S. Eliot wrote his *Murder in the Cathedral* for the Canterbury Festivals; Canterbury may still be considered as the most adequate place for staging the play. Christopher Fry wrote his *Sleep of Prisoners* for production in churches. Although a church setting can be erected on any stage, it makes a difference if the audience does not only see the church on the stage but sits in it. A more spurious adaptation of plays to a particular place of performance is the choice of an historical setting for an historical play as, for example, performances of Schiller's *Wallenstein* in Eger (1939) or Goethe's *Goetz von Berlichingen* in Jagsthausen. On the other hand, when producing *Winterreise* with texts from Hölderlin's *Hyperion* as a play on the tragic dilemma of German History in the Olympic stadium of Berlin - built under Hitler for the games in 1936 - on a December evening of 1977, Klaus Michael Grueber achieved a most singularly symbolic effect.

Another matter is the choice of an open air theatre as the place of production. The open air theatre may either provide a neutral setting for the performance of any play or a setting particularly fitting to the action of a play. But producing Rossini's *Barbiere di Siviglia* in a park theatre (Eutin 1976) does not make much sense as you have to reconstruct a town in that park.

3.2. Stage

The choice of a particular place for the production of a play usually includes the choice of a particular stage as well. A particular stage may be implied on the dramatic text for various reasons. A very simple stage may suffice for amateur production as long as the audience does not expect the perfection it is used to in professional performances.

The early Aeschylus expected nothing but an empty platform. Up to his *Prometheus Bound* his dramatic texts imply, in contradistinction to later plays, nothing but an open countryside unflanked by any building. His later plays imply the existence of a stage-house ("skene"), and many plays of Euripides - and Aristophanes, in parody of his contemporary - already imply a considerable amount of machinery. A god could not appear on the top of a palace roof in the dramatic text before a "skene" was part of the stage. Either the playwright adapted his play to the possibilities of the stage or the stage was adapted to new plays.

Scenes on the battlement of a castle as in Shakespeare's *Hamlet* or on a balcony as in his *Romeo and Juliet* imply a stage providing a raised level for staging as the Globe theatre did. The medieval mystery play needed a three-level stage to represent heaven, earth, and hell. The same provisions that apply to the arrangement of action on different levels also apply to the arrangement of action in depth. The text may imply that the scene may open into another room. Aeschylus' text of his *Oresteia*, for example, cannot rely on such an arrangement. The murder of Agamemnon is registered only from the outside. Euripides' and Aristophanes' texts already imply an "ekkuklema", a low platform that could be swung out of one of the stage-doors of the "skene" to expose interiors. A further development in the adaptation of interior scenes may be seen in the curtained inner stage of the Elizabethan theatre.

The depth of the stage must be seen in connection with its shape and its position in relation to the auditorium. Greek tragedy needed a proscenium for the action and an orchestra for the chorus. Elizabethan drama usually implied a platform stage. Realistic drama is in most cases conceived of as being performed on a four-wall stage. Japanese Nô-plays, as well as a number of modern plays, need gangways or scaffolds extending the stage into the auditorium. Performances like that of Klaus Michael Gruber's adaptation of Hölderlin's *Empedokles* for the Berlin Schaubühne 1975 even use two parallel stages for parallel actions. Jerome Savary may use the whole theatre as a stage for his *Grand Magic Circus*.

Scenes with limited interiors such as caves or small cottages are difficult to enact on stages that are too large. For purposes like these the size of the stage could be changed during the performance. The designer for the 1976 production of Frank Wedekind's *Frühlings Erwachen* in Munich, Hans Kleber, cut off the larger part of the stage for the interior of the poor Bergmanns; he opened the stage into the stage-house for the last scene on the churchyard.

To a large extent the production does not merely depend upon the implications of the dramatic text. What may be the stage as implied in the text, could be considered as inadequate at a later period. The multiplicity of scenes in Elizabethan drama implied a comparatively empty stage. An audience used to realistic settings and expecting them needs a stage to provide multiple settings or the possibility of a quick change of scenery and a curtain in addition to hide it. As theatre and stage are not fixed but only implied by the text, they are much more likely to change than the language of the text. The play is normally adapted to the place of performance and its stage in the form in which they are available. This is true with regard to stage tradition in general, of which place of production and stage are only parts.

3.3. Production.

Actually we should not talk of stage tradition only but of the art of producing a play, of which, again, tradition is only part. We have the art of writing a play and the art of its adequate production. The art of production involves interpretation of the text as well as the use of dramatic means to realize it on the stage. In the following paragraphs we will examine the dramatic means such as setting, costume, and acting.

3.3.1. Setting. The stage setting may or may not be described by the playwright. If the author does not use stage-directions, he usually relies on stage convention or takes part in directing the play. The setting of the first production usually has authoritative character, will be used in later productions, and may become a tradition. This is the case even in the modern theatre as the imitation of Joe Mielziner's setting for Tennessee Williams' *A Streetcar Named Desire* in many later productions, for example, proves. The stage directions may be laid down with co-operation between author and director during rehearsal. The result of such a co-operation has, in the modern American theatre, become the acting version, available for the producer, besides the normal reading version for sale in bookshops.

The stage direction may be rather short, just indicating exterior or interior, or it may describe the setting in all its details. Examples of very detailed description of stage settings are the plays by Eugene O'Neill. In the case of detailed stage directions, it can be presumed that the author considers them as implied by his text. The stage director or designer may be of a different opinion and still consider a different setting as adequate to the dramatic text. He has the greater authority because of his experience on the stage. He can usually calculate the effect on the audience better than the author. He has to take into account the expectations of the audience which usually are directed by what it is used to seeing on the stage. To disappoint the audience in its expectations may, on the one hand, block an adequate understanding of the play. On the other hand, satisfying the expectations may associate the meaning of the play with that of former plays using the same kind of setting and may not allow the play to get a new message across. No rule can be established for the preference of the one or the other way to meet the expectation of the audience. It usually depends on the originality of the dramatic text itself.

The setting may be implied in the dramatic text in different ways. It may be referred to by the characters in the play, it may be put down in stage directions, as already mentioned, or it may be implied in a more general way by the action. Allusions to locality by the characters of the play need not necessarily refer to stage settings. On the contrary they are usually meant to stimulate the imagination of the audience. Hippolytus' opening monologue in Seneca's *Phaedra* describes the scenery of his hunting in many details. We do not know if it was ever produced on the stage of the author's time. The Roman theatre was able to provide painted screens for such purposes. But Hippolytus' description was probably only to be meant to stimulate the imagination of Seneca's readers. In Shakespeare's plays "word-scenery" as imaginary scenery supplants actual scenery. Or the other way round, because scenic settings are missing the playwright creates the illusion of them in his spoken text. The more the stage makes use of realistic settings, the less it becomes necessary for the characters to talk about the scenery. Actually the play becomes more a work of stage art and less literary, once the text is relieved of the necessity to provide for imaginary scenery.

The stage setting normally depends on period style and available conveniences. Part of the setting is usually provided by constituents of the stage as the "skene" of the Greek theatre, or balcony and inner stage of the public theatre in Elizabethan England. Classical style may, as in the case of seventeenth century French tragedy, be reflected in more or less fixed settings imitating Greek or Roman architecture. A most marvellous reconstruction of a fixed stage setting can be seen in Jean-Pierre Ponelle's Zurich production of Monteverdi's *L'Orfeo, L'Incoronazione di Poppea,* and *Il Ritorno d'Ulisse in Patria,* using the same setting for all three operas (1975 - 1977). Realistic or naturalistic style usually is reflected in detailed settings. The range of possibilities extends from the bare stage of the Elizabethan theatre to the realism of the nineteenth century stage.

In addition to the bare stage, to fixed and realistic settings, other stylized settings are possible. Stylizition may be achieved for different purposes by stage decoration not representing but alluding to realistic details, by selective realism, symbolic realism, symbolic stage properties, or the use of light. It is also possible to use settings not reflecting the scenery implied but either representing nothing but decoration or suggesting a larger context in which the play may be seen. For example, the setting for Kleist's *Prinz von Homburg,* designed in 1972 by Wilfried Minks for the production at the Schiller Theater in Berlin, consists of an oversized statue of a kneeling angel with his hands on the floor as if trying to protect somebody, and consequently interprets the play in the context of man's general plight. A similar effect is achieved if a particularized historical scene is acted before the background of a different time.

Finally, another possibility which should be mentioned is that the stage be left completely bare, as is often done - according to the playwright's own instructions - in productions of plays by Bertolt Brecht, and also by authors like Thornton Wilder or Luigi Pirandello: The play becomes transparent as an illusion.

Parallel to what was said about the language used in the dramatic text, it is possible to distinguish three basic functions of the setting as far as its contemporaneity is concerned. It may reflect the time of the action within the play, the time of its first production, or the time of any later period. If the setting is supposed to reflect a former time, it does not depend so much on historical correctness as on the conception the audience has of that time. If it considers it similar to its own, no historical setting is necessary.

A particular effect can be achieved if the production tries to come as close as possible to the original first production, that is, not to find a setting best fitting to its text, but rather one that characterizes the period of its author. It may, as the production of Richard Wagner's *Tannhäuser*, directed by Hans-Peter Liebermann in Munich, expose the romanticism of its author. Hans Hollmann reached far beyond the original text when he created a nineteenth century middle-class setting as a frame for his production of the same composer's *Rheingold* in Basel to expose its composer's psyche.

3.3.2. Costume. Costumes may be considered as part of the setting. As in the case of stage decoration they may be prescribed by the author's stage directions. Acting on a bare stage corresponds to acting in costumes of the time of production. Acting in a realistic setting asks for a realistic dressing corresponding to the decorations. But period style, implications of the dramatic text, and/or the stage director's interpretation allow all possible variations. While contemporary dressing was the rule on the stage from the Middle Ages until the late eighteenth century, audiences of the following periods expected performances in historical costumes.

The same effect as that created by setting up the stage decorations in view of the audience is achieved by the actors dressing on the stage. Both are alienation effects. But alienation may also be achieved by contemporary dressing in historical plays if the audience is used to expecting historical costumes. If Faust in Goethe's play does not appear in medieval costume but in that of the author's time he does the same as the designer does with the corresponding setting mentioned above. On the modern stage, present-day dressing for historical plays has quite a different effect from Shakespeare's time because the audience has become accustomed to historical dressing.

An equivalent to symbolic stage properties is to be seen in symbolic dressing. Symbolic dressing may comprise simple attributes, such as a crown marking its bearer as king. Or it may be as elaborate as in Japanese Nô-plays. While modern symbolic dressing usually is designed for the production of a particular play, traditional symbolic costumes of former times, as in the Japanese Nô-play or the Peking opera, usually carry fixed meanings. A fixed kind of costume is also used for typification, the best known example being that of the harlequin in the Italian commedia dell'arte.

Stylized dressing often goes together with the use of masks as in Greek drama, Japanese Nô-plays, or in commedia dell'arte. Besides its allegorizing, symbolizing, or typifying function, it may expose the illusionary character of the actor's impersonation.

3.3.3. Acting. Most of what was said about setting and costume can be applied to acting, therefore it is not necessary to go into the details of its possibilities for adapting the dramatic text. Acting involves the way of speaking the text, facial expression and gesture accompanying it, and the movement of the characters on the stage. A production may use the acting conventions of the time when the play was written or those of its own time. Acting a play according to the rules of its own time may have a rather modern effect of abstraction if its production does not meet the expectation of the audience. This was the case with a recent Munich production of Molière's early *Les Fourberies de Scapin* in commedia dell'arte manner.

Parallel to setting and costume acting may imitate life realistically, it may expose itself as fictive, it may be ritualized, or it may be stylized in many different ways.

Acting may use all the means enumerated above; it may stress the one or the other, or limit itself to one or two of them. For example, traditional opera makes hardly any use of moving on the stage, whereas pantomime does not use speech. Furthermore, pantomime can be acted according to a dramatic text and express the meaning of its words in gestures and in movements, possibly for special purposes such as a performance before a deaf audience.

Though settings and acting are means to actualize a written text it may happen that a text is only used by the designer or actor to demonstrate his own art. As long as he considers his art as a means of actualizing the text it may be perfectly in accordance with the intentions of the author. Shakespeare probably wrote passages with Richard Burbage or Kemp in mind. Tennessee Williams considered Anna Magnana as the best actress for the Serafina of his *Rose Tatoo*. A rather singular case is Thomas Bernhard's *Minetti* written for the actor Minetti. But acting is going beyond its original purpose in star-performances arranged to produce the actor and not the play. The same may happen to the art of the designer as in Peter Stein's recent production of Shakespeare's *As You Like It* for which he turned a large hall of a Berlin film studio into a vast symbolical landscape. Acting as movement may be developed into the art of choreography. Like pantomime or dance it is able to do without a written text. The adaptation of a dramatic text then becomes a translation of an idea from the medium of one art to that of another.

4. INTERPRETATION.

The last examples make it obvious that it is difficult to draw definite border lines between one art and the other. Actually we have a whole range of arts, each defined as occupying a sector of the range, the sectors overlapping or being combined with each other. The unique position of drama within the framework of the arts is characterized by its possibility to include all the other arts as a "Gesamtkunstwerk" on the one hand, and by depending on literature and one of the performing arts to be fully realized on the other. The participation of other arts raises the question of subordination. As long as our subject is drama it may be said that they are to be considered as subsidiary and to be evaluated according to their contribution to the realization of the dramatic text on the stage. The dependence on both literature, i.e. the dramatic text, and one of the performing arts, i.e. its realization on the stage, raises the question of actualization. The text, considered as literature, and therefore fixed for all time in this form, has to be realized in an art which finds its expression in its performance only. The hermeneutic problem involved is that principally two ways of communication are possible. The one would be to realize the text on the stage as close as possible to the original conception the author may have had in mind. In this case the spectator would receive the play according to his own experience, and this experience would necessarily be different from that of the author. The other way would be to adapt the text to a performance in accordance with the experience of the audience. The interpretation of the text through the performance would eliminate the hermeneutical divergence. Both possibilities involve interpretation: in the one case, that of what the author actually intended to communicate, in the other, that of what the audience's communication level really is.

4.1. Contemporary Plays.

The problem of diverging interpretation does not only rise with older plays but with contemporary plays as well. For example, it becomes apparent if the play was written for a different kind of audience from that for which it is produced. In this case either the author may adapt his text for the particular audience or the dramatic advisor or stage-manager may interpret it on the stage in terms of his audience. To a certain extent this will be necessary for every play as the stage-manager may be more familiar with the possibilities of communication with his audience than its writer. For that reason the final text of Broadway plays sometimes do not get fixed before the opening night. It sometimes happens that the author withdraws his play because what he intended to communicate does not seem to be conveyed by the performance.

4.2. Rewriting.

The adaptation of a dramatic text to the performance may involve changes. If the changes involve variations in meaning it would be better to talk of rewriting. Shakespeare's *Hamlet* probably was a rewriting of an *Urhamlet*. In this case the author may have considered his version to be a better interpretation of the historical Hamlet-story. Throughout the history of drama this has often been a reason for rewriting plays. Sophocles and Euripides wrote their *Electra* at about the same time, each being a different interpretation of the Electra-myth. Hofmannsthal or Giraudoux wrote their versions of the myth for our century. Many other examples could be quoted. A different way of rewriting a story would be to adapt it to a different period of history, as O'Neill did when he transferred this myth into nineteenth century America in his *Mourning Becomes Electra*. The conviction that the story can no longer be interpreted in our time even may be subject of a later play as in Heiner Müller's phantasmogoria *Die Hamletmaschine* (1977) in the manner of Artaud's "theatre of cruelty". Rewriting is, strictly speaking, not the interpretation of a dramatic text, but the interpretation of its story or its subject. It must be pointed out, however, that, in this context, the interpretation of an older play in a contemporary production may come very close to the production of a new play based on the same story or the same subject.

Between rewriting the text for present-day purposes and translating and adapting it to the level of present-day communication, there are a number of texts offering alternatives of interpretation by the author, for example, Goethe's *Stella* and Tennessee Williams' *Cat on a Hot Tin Roof*. The different endings of these plays imply different interpretations of the story. The stage-manager may even combine the different versions of the author as it is, for example, being done in productions of Goethe's play: The earlier version, with its happy ending, is presented as the dream of the dying Stella of the later version. Another possibility is represented by Goethe's two versions of his *Iphigenie auf Tauris*, the one written in prose, the other in verse. The stage-manager is even more at liberty, if the text he is going to produce is handed down as a fragment. In this case the production actually has to supplement or rather complete the text and sometimes even has to supply an interpretation of the story. Examples would be Hölderlin's *Empedokles*, Büchner's *Woyzeck*, or Alban Berg's opera *Lulu* based on plays by Wedekind. One reason that they are produced so often may be the present-day stage-manager's desire to be as free in his interpretation as possible.

4.3. Older Plays.

As far as contemporary plays are concerned the interpretations of the text as well as of the audience reaction by the author and by the stage-manager may differ but they are to be considered to move on the same level of communication. Rewriting allows translation of the story to a later level of communication either in its original or in a different historical particularization. The existence of different versions allows the choice of the one closer to present-day understanding.

If only one version of an older text exists, it may be produced to effect, as close as possible, either the level of communication it experienced with its original audience, or the level of communication the text offers a modern audience. The different levels of communication usually imply different levels of interpretation as well.

4.3.1. Interpretation by the Audience.

Producing an older play according to the original interpretation is practically impossible. The older the play, the more difficult it becomes to reconstruct its original interpretation. Even if it could be reconstructed, it might no longer be meaningful to a modern audience. If it is found worthy of production in our time, the general assumption is that the text as a work of art is "timeless", meaning that it contains something that is common to the interpretations of the time of its author and the time of a present-day spectator. As long as that "imaginary" common denominator can still be recognized by a modern audience, the production may keep comparatively close to the original text and can make do with the minimum of translation and adaptation in the sense elaborated above. The play's level of communication with its modern audience, then, will be similar to that with its original audience with all the paraphernalia peculiar to its own time still intact and still meaningful. Recognizing what is common to that earlier time and his own time the spectator is usually able to translate the paraphernalia of the one period into those of his own and to interpret them accordingly. Often the paraphernalia imply consequences of different importance for their respective audience. The major difference in interpretation will depend on the experience mankind was able to acquire or lose in the meantime. Because of these implications the common denominator of the different interpretations may be an "imaginary" one, i.e. we only imagine, or hope, that the original audience could interpret the play as we do.

A production still is on the same level of interpretation if it stresses or isolates one or part of different levels of meaning in a play. Other levels of meaning may no longer be relevant, the play may be too long for a present-day production, or it may be the particular intention of the production to communicate these meanings only. An example would be productions of *Hamlet* cutting references to Fortinbras and Norway. In this case the interpretation would concentrate on the personal tragedy of Hamlet and exclude its political implications.

4.3.2. Interpretation by the Performance. Production of older plays on the level of a modern audience's interpretation of the text still implies an "imaginary" common denominator. But as the production on the level of the original audience assumes that the common denominator can still be recognized, the production on the level of a modern audience assumes that it was recognized already by a former audience. The text produced is no longer something which is still valid, but something that had also been valid before. It is no longer an interpretation of former life, but an interpretation of present-day life with the help of a former interpretation.

There may be different reasons for the preference for one over the other interpretation. It may be simply the question of preponderance of the one or the other art, the art of literature or the art of performing. The producer may consider his audience too lacking in critical ability to recognize the relevance of the text to today's life. Or, attaching more significance to its social function than to its aesthetic effect, he may consider it better realized by his modern interpretation. In all these cases the task of the audience to recognize the common denominator is usurped or taken over by the production. The reinterpretation of the text in terms of present-day life is no longer to be done by the spectator but is done by the performance. Production of an older play in terms of our time then allows greater immediacy of reception and comprehension but also limits the possibilities of interpretation. The direct application of the original text by the reader or spectator to present-day relevance makes a larger range of interpretations possible. Each spectator may interpret it differently. The application by production more or less limits its application to that of the stage-manager. The more individualistic the spectator is, the less he will be inclined to accept the interpretation by the production. For the same reason, actualization of a play by way of its interpretation through production may easily become the handmaid of indoctrination, allowing the one interpretation of the stage-manager to achieve its effect through the experience of immediacy.

The production of a play in terms of present-day interpretation can use a maximum of translation and adaptation of the text to the present-day level either of communication or of alienation, but will usually combine both possibilities. The assumption in the first case is that the play could be produced as if it were written today. In the second case alienation effects expose what may be considered as dated by the audience and bring home what is relevant to its present-day situation.

The basis of interpretation for text and production will principally differ from individual to individual. Nevertheless the presuppositions underlying the individual interpretations can be generalized according to various points of view. Principally they may be considered as depending upon the conceptions of art, man and the world shared by social groups at a particular time. Different and changing conceptions call forth other and new interpretations of the play. The original text of an older play may be based on idiosyncrasies of its time. In this case it probably will be forgotten very soon. It may be based on conceptions which - perhaps not accepted in its own time - become important in the future development of art and thinking and which are - at least partly - still acceptable for a later period. An older text based on the idiosyncrasies of a particular time may be rediscovered by a later period sharing the same idiosyncrasies. Then it would be possible to present it according to its original interpretation or to that of a later period. But the older play based on presuppositions still valid at a later period will have limitations if presented in terms of the idiosyncrasies of a later period. For this reason production would be foolish to follow fashion rather than dramatic texts which can always easily be compared with older texts and evaluated accordingly. Though film documentation of production opens up new possibilities for comparing produtions of different periods, the history of the stage is something quite different from that of the dramatic text. The question the audience usually asks is: What did the author intend to get across with his play and what does it mean to me? Knowing the written text a spectator may also ask, if the stage-manager sees the play the same way as he sees it. A sophisticated audience may even be interested in seeing a production interpreting the play in terms not of the original but of an intermediate period.

To a certain extent stage production may be seen on the same level as a contemporary play. It may serve a purpose limited to its particular time. The production as well as the play may be forgotten if that time has past. The ideal production of any play, contemporary or written in an earlier period, could, for these reasons, be seen in an interpretation which will - at least "imaginarily" - be accepted by an audience of any period. In such a case the interpretations of author, stage-manager, and audience would converge. Particularities depending on the different factors would have to be generalized. Such a production can only be conceived of as an "idea" and probably has never been performed nor will ever be in the future. Yet, it may serve as a point of departure to define the position of actual realization of drama on the stage. But even this "ideal" realization can - in the case of older plays - only be an "imaginary" one, because interpretations of different times can never be identical.

5. CONCLUSION

Dramatic art has so far been considered as a mixed art, considering the dramatic text as literature and the production as a performing art. It is, of course, possible to consider the dramatic text as literature only. Actually this is the way it has predominantly been done in the past. It is meaningful if the literary qualities of the text are the main object of interest. Of other texts, e.g., closed dramas, it may be said that they are written in the form of a dramatic text either not intended for the stage or not suited to it, as Shelley's *Prometheus Unbound* or Tieck's *Genoveva*.

The question is not definitely settled if Seneca's tragedies were written for reading, declamation or acting. Other literary texts, as for example, dramatic monologues, may show dramatic elements but not be conceived of as drama.

In the same way stage performance may be considered as performing art only. It becomes rather questionable if, for example, Peter Zadek's performances of Shakespeare's plays can be considered as interpretations of the author's text. Nevertheless the performance may be a meaningful play in its own right or an original interpretation of the story Shakespeare used for his play. In cases such as this, the production writes its own text or imposes its own interpretation of a story on the interpretation formulated in a different text. The extreme possibility is that of the "absolute theatre", (playwright, director, and actor represented in one person), as Antonin Artaud had it in mind, or co-operating in producing a play, as it is done by experiments in group dynamics, for example the "group-project" *Atlantis* at the Bochum playhouse in 1976, managed by Augosto Fernandos. To a certain extent they establish a text for the production. The last step toward "absolute theatre" would be creating a new text for each performance, the text coming into being with the performance only. "Theatre", then, as Artaud formulated it, "is in truth the history of creation". As the text can be seen in the context of literature, the performance can be seen in that of the other performing arts; dramatic performance may take recourse on any of the performing arts or any combination of them.

If we are correct to assume that drama developed out of ritual, the performing art must have developed from ritual dance and literature from the dramatized text of scripture. Wherever drama is something other than ritual, it has to be considered as something consisting of both. All artistic interpretation is subject to historical change. Through the "imaginary" common denominator of interpretation, a play may be produced as belonging to all time. But it must always be interpreted as belonging to the time in which it was originally conceived or to the time in which it is performed. Because of its unique position within the framework of the arts, drama may be considered as perhaps the most interesting art, for it offers a range of possibilities in realization, communication, and interpretation, only part of which could be covered by the present paper.

CHAPTER 5

Transcending Culture: A Cantonese Translation and Production of O'Neill's *Long Day's Journey into Night*

VICKI C. H. OOI

> *... it is not possible to conceive of a person standing beyond his culture. His culture has brought him into being in every respect except the physical, and given him his categories and habits of thought, his range of feeling, his idiom and tones of speech.* [1]

Anyone familiar with O'Neill's plays would immediately agree that what Lionel Trilling said about culture and art applies precisely to O'Neill's works. All his plays reflect his cultural background and his experiences which emerged from his New England Irish Catholic background. *Long Day's Journey into Night*, O'Neill's most personal play, is indeed subject to this cultural restriction. It is informed by the family culture, a particular kind of New England Irish Catholicism which provides the feelings and mores of the play, its character types and their inter-relationships. The whole pervading attitude towards life in general comes from this provincial life style. [2]

The strong sense and "feel" of New England Catholicism is largely responsible for creating the tensions and paradoxes in *Long Day's Journey*. The fluctuations in James Tyrone's character spring from the tension between his neurotic fear of the poor-house, a neurosis stemming from his childhood poverty in Ireland, and his own natural generosity. Mary is torn between the Irish religious ideal of virginal chastity and the reality of marriage to a down-to-earth Irishman with raw passions and an insatiable taste for alcohol and bar-room humour. The tension between delicate sentiment and beauty on the one hand and brutality and grossness on the other is reflected in the schizophrenic behaviour of both Jamie and Edmund who vacillate between their delicate sensibility for their family and their coarse, drunken expeditions to the local whorehouse. This same essential paradox finds expression in the poetry of the Anglo-Irish decadents and in Baudelaire's poetry which is quoted frequently by the characters in the plays and which O'Neill weaves into the play as an integral part.

How then can this feel of O'Neill's background,which informs the play and which forms the prism through which we view the preoccupations of the writer and his characters,be transposed into another language and culture? The intrinsic aspects of a culture, with its traditional emphases and reservations, are intimately bound up with its language and are, to a certain extent, incommunicable. Therefore, when a language is utilized in literature there are latent cultural insights evoked by the language - a kind of " ... rehabilitation of the memory that exists in words." [3] In this respect, any translation of *Long Day's Journey* is bound to fail: for no matter how accurate the translation may be technically, it is bound to lose this precise cultural "feel" which gives the play its inner tension. The reader in his study can always provide himself with the necessary background information to the play, but the producer, unlike the teacher of literature, cannot expect his audience to do this. Programme notes, though helpful, will always only be programme notes - at best erudite and informative but never good enough to bring about the shared response between dramatist, actors and audience that is possible when the language of the play is the language of the culture of the playgoers.

It is, however, possible to make the best of this inevitable loss. One can argue that, in accepting the limitations of the foreigner to penetrate all the recesses of an alien culture and to catch the characteristic modes and subtle intonations of its attendant language, the translator is opening himself to the fascination of experiencing " ...the irreducibly singular, the idiosyncratic, that gives every literature its own beauty and its enigma". [4]

Lionel Trilling (1965) sums up the relationship between culture and literature succinctly and most perceptively:

> *It is a belief still pre-eminently honoured that a primary function of art and thought is to liberate the individual from the tyranny of his culture in the environmental sense and to permit him to stand beyond it in an autonomy of perception and judgement.* [5]

Trilling was not writing about the problems of translation, but what he said applies aptly to the problems of translating a play like *Long Day's Journey*, one which is so profoundly steeped in its own culture for an audience which is equally rigidly fixed in its own culture. The task of the translator is not to render his work so that it becomes immediately familiar to his own people, but to maintain the "strangeness" or "foreignness" of the original work. He does this by conveying the particular state of mind of the artist and by revealing the unexpected insights and unaccustomed feelings implicit in the work. The translation must be a discovery to the translator as well as to his readers. *Long Day's Journey* must be translated as a fine and precise document about a family set in a New England Irish background and if this is achieved, it will help us all to move, in one instance, closer to Arnold's ideal - "every critic should try to possess one great literature, at least, beside his own; and the more unlike his own, the better".[6]

With two or three literatures open to him, the critic is equipped to draw various relationships, to judge; with two cultures open to them the audience of a play can at least hope to re-evaluate the values of their own culture if not that of the foreign culture which they are made to confront. In the case of *Long Day's Journey*, the cross-cultural problems are less difficult and more urgent, since the play is to be read not only as a cultural or sociological document, but as a dramatization of tensions arising within a family bound by resentment and guilt and held by love and concern. These tensions, of course, have parallels in Chinese literature and in Chinese life.

The mores and inner relationships of the family have preoccupied Chinese writers ever since *The Dream of the Red Chamber* and after the Chinese Revolution of 1919 the family became an open target of attack: the young revolutionaries saw it as a symbol of the iniquitous old feudal system which had to be swept away. Writing about his trilogy of novels, *Turbulent Spring*, Pa Chin, one of the leading modern Chinese writers, spoke for his generation when he said:

> *I did not want simply to write the history of our family. What I wanted to write had to be the history of a typical feudal family. Its main characters had to be those whom we constantly saw in such families.* 7

and again:

> *I wanted to show how those families (typical families like those described in the trilogy) inevitably go down the road to ruin, how they dig their own graves with their own hands. I wanted to describe the inner struggles and tragedies inside these families ... how lovable youths suffer there, how they struggle and finally do not escape destruction. At the end I wanted to personify in him my hope. I wanted him to bring fresh air to us ... In those families we do not have much fresh air.* [8]

Since at the time when Pa Chin was writing, the idea of family was so closely related to notions of the oppression of individual freedom, Pa Chin, and others like him, wrote in a spirit of rebellion. Writing became for them the most effective way of uttering their <j'accuse> against the family which symbolized the whole feudal system. In his trilogy, Pa Chin delineates the tyranny of the patriarchal system, showing how the head of the family runs his family: the grandfather or the father of the house decides the education and careers of his children and grandchildren who have no say whatever in any of the decisions which affect their lives. Even marriages are made by the patriarch - sometimes at his own eccentric whim. His word is law and all are obliged to carry out his wishes. Trained to obey him without question, members of the family submit in silence or with sullen surrender to the patriarch's tyrannical sway. But the younger people belonging to Pa Chin's generation, influenced by new changes, refused to submit. They rose in revolt against the tyranny of the system. Hence, the suffering of those who submit to the system, and the heroism of those brave enough to defy it, form the central contrast in a large number of novels and plays written in this era. The preoccupation of and attitudes taken by writers like Pa Chin are understandable, but this overtly polemical attitude imposes a kind of rigidity on the language in their works. In describing the tensions which arise when the old harshly impose their authority on the young who either cringe in submission or who fight back with a vengeance, the language used is one either of sullen acceptance or of attack and rebellion. The language is unambiguously polarized,just as the attitudes of the oppressor and the oppressed are polarized. Tenderness and concern are found only among the oppressed, and no tenderness is found between the oppressors and the victims.

A chasm separates them - a psychological and a linguistic gulf.

In a novel, the gap between what is actually spoken and what is felt can still be bridged by descriptions of people's unexpressed feelings and can so partly soften this polarity. But in drama a great deal more depends on the language used on stage. Ts'ao Yu, one of the leading modern Chinese dramatists, dramatized Pa Chin's *Family* (the first part of the trilogy). His dramatic version, which retains the flavour of Pa Chin's language, provides an interesting example of this polarization of hatred and rebellion in action and in language.

Here is a scene in which Feng, the lecherous friend of the grandfather of the Kao family, sadistically burns his maid's hand with his lighted cigarette in order to intimidate her and prevent her from telling the Kao family the sordid truth about the sexual abuse she received in Feng's house. The young grandson, seeing this, rises in protest against the old man.

CHUEH-HUI (roughly) *Let go of her! What are you trying to do?*

FENG (stunned speechless) *You. You .....*

CHUEH-HUI (in a rage) *Why are you torturing her?*

FENG *Who ... who's torturing her?*

CHUEH-HUI *God, you're shameless. Still trying to cover up? Don't you see the pain she's in?* (bitterly) *You hypocrite! You mere semblance of a gentleman! Putting on such a show of virtue in front of the young.*

YUAN-YI (the maid) *Third master!*

FENG (finally finds his voice, shakily) *You ... you have no respect for your elders or betters.*

CHUEH-HUI (staring Feng in the face) *I have no respect for you, and my fists have no respect for you either. I'm not going to waste my breath on you, I want you to set Yuan-yi free.*

FENG (slowly regaining his cool haughty composure) *You uncouth youngster. Even if you are ignorant of the disciplines of a family, you should know something of the law of the country.*

CHUEH-HUI *Huh! The laws of the country do not protect the likes of you!*

FENG (disdainfully) *You're uncouth and uneducated. I shan't bother with you. In a moment I shall tell your grandfather to teach you some discipline.*

CHUEH-HUI (catches a glimpse of his grandfather coming) *My grandfather is here, I hope you tell him!*

FENG *Huh!* (sullenly)

KAO (sees Feng standing there staring, smiles) *Venerable Master Feng, meditating again? What excellent lines have you come up with now?* (raising the book of poetry he is carrying) *Your poetry is truly admirable! Every word a gem!*

FENG (disconcerted) *You're too generous.*

CHUEH-HUI *Grand-uncle, didn't you say you were going to tell grandfather ...*

KAO (interested) *Tell me what? Are you pondering for the best word?*

FENG (in suppressed rage, but trying to pass it off as a smile) *Oh, nothing, ... nothing much. Just a slight difference of opinion over a few words.*

KAO *Venerable Master Feng, do you know, the students are making trouble again,* (turning around) *Ke-ming, didn't you say just now that the students here are holding some kind of meeting again ... some patriotic demonstration or other ...*

MING (respectfully) *Yes, sir.*

KAO (rhetorically) *"Traitors and thieves, he who finds them has a right to kill them."*

FENG (menacingly) *Has a right to kill them, indeed.*

KAO (to Hui) *What are you standing here for? Why don't you leave us?*

HUI *Yes.* 9

The confrontation is clearly a dramatic one as Ts'ao Yu dramatizes the head-on collision of two generations who are unwilling to give way to each other. But because the attitudes are already so firmly set, with Chueh-hui cast in the role of the heroic young rebel taking on the Venerable Master Feng who is cast as the hypocritical and tyrannical patriarch of the loathed feudal system, the confrontation is no more than a celebration of a glorious rebellion. No attempt is made to search for an understanding and although both sides suffer from the wounds inflicted in the verbal battle, no self-knowledge is gained. Consequently the language takes on the set and rigid quality of the attitudes of the speakers: there is no probing, no ambiguity. It seems like dialogue written to William Archer's doctrine: the characters speak "in character", and speeches are economical and even the timing is faultless. But if one may quote Pinter, the language used is not "a language where under what is said another thing is being said". In other words, there is no subtext, which is, as defined by Stanislavski, the man who invented this term, "a web of innumerable, varied inner patterns under a play ..." Similarly, we see the same set attitudes in the most intimate and anguished dialogue between Jui, the wife of Chueh-hsin, and Mei, the girl he loved but was not allowed to marry:

JUI *Let me finish.* (tears roll down her cheeks) *I've wanted so many times, to go home to my mother ...*

MEI (shocked) *You ...*

JUI *... and hand over both him and Hai-yi to you ...*

MEI (in grief) *Cousin-in-law, you really don't know what you are saying. I ... I've to go.*

JUI (sadly but eagerly) *Cousin Mei, his life is really miserable. It makes my heart ache to see him suffer like this.* (pleadingly) *You don't find me silly, I hope. There is nobody in this family who really loves him. I know that you understand him and love him. That is why I feel that you'll understand what I'm saying.*

MEI (sadly) *Cousin-in-law, what is there to understand?*

JUI *I ... I really love him.*

MEI (bows her head) *I know, cousin-in-law.*

JUI *No, you haven't quite understood. I love him truly, so inexpressibly. Such love. I'm only happy when he is happy. But he is so sad, so sad! He hasn't really laughed happily, not once. That is why, Cousin Mei, I thought ...*

MEI *What did you think?*

JUI *I thought of saying what I did ...*

MEI *That you ...*

JUI (in earnest) *You may not believe it, but I am serious. I'm not saying this to please or flatter ... It's not a pose. You will understand that a woman can love her husband to distraction, and is prepared to forget everything about herself.*

MEI (frankly) *Cousin-in-law, you are fortunate. It is true happiness to be able to marry and love one's husband so.*

JUI (in earnest) *Think, Cousin Mei, you're leaving us. For his sake, and for your own sake ...*

MEI (smiles sadly) *Don't joke about it.*

JUI (in earnest) *I'm not joking.*

MEI (watching Yue and slowly shaking her head) *Then, won't you suffer when you leave him?*

JUI (suppressing herself) *eh ... no.*

MEI *When your family sees you coming home, won't they suffer?*

JUI (bows her head and frowns) *eh ... no.*

MEI (her voice shaking) *Won't Hai-yi suffer without you?*

JUI (quivering) *eh ... eh.*

MEI *Won't you suffer when you leave Hai-yi?*

JUI (breaks down crying) *I'll suffer, I'll suffer! But what other way is there? I can't bear to see him suffering like this any more!*

MEI (pitying her) *Cousin-in-law, there is no end to suffering. You think too much.* 10

The scene is moving, but again there is no probing, no tension, because there is no subtext. The dialogue is an expression of resolved attitudes, not an attempt to show an attitude in the process of being resolved in front of the audience. We see two women ready to sacrifice their lives for the happiness of the man they love - but the spirit of self-sacrifice, moving though it is, is a set heroic attitude and allows for no complexity in the language.

Of all the modern Chinese dramatists, Ts'ao Yu has probably the surest hand in using dramatic language to express feelings in those areas of the psyche which are irrational. He comes closest to using language to explore self-knowledge especially in his women characters, as we see in the exchange between Chueh-hsin's wife and Cousin Mei here, and also in glimpses of his heroines Fan-yi (in *Thunderstorm*) and Chin-tzu (in *The Wilderness*). Unfortunately this exploration of the self through dramatic language is almost always fragmentary and is soon submerged in a welter of larger social concerns in Ts'ao Yu's plays. It never became the central and exclusive concern of his plays and so Ts'ao Yu never took full advantage of his genius, his capacity to blend the polarized violence and tenderness, as did O'Neill, to create the kind of complex subtextual tension that leads to probing and discovery. This kind of subtextual tension is the characteristic of *Long Day's Journey* and consequently *Long Day's Journey* is such a challenge to the translator. Its subtextual ambiguity and multiple tonality are still new to us in Hong Kong. It is new even to an audience used to Ts'ao Yu's plays. O'Neill's play makes its greatest demands in the area in which the language of modern Chinese drama has been least developed.

In *Long Day's Journey*, the Tyrones reach self-knowledge and understanding and acceptance in their long day's journey only because of their capacity for honesty, a capacity which finally overcomes the instinct to hide behind recrimination and self-justification. And for once O'Neill finds a language to convey the pain, the understanding and the forgiveness - a language simple in its naturalism and yet strong enough to carry the attendant emotional undertones. O'Neill was being modest when he made Edmund deprecate his ability to convey his dreams to his father and to us:

> *I couldn't touch what I tried to tell you just now. I just stammered. That's the best I'll ever do ... Well, it'll be faithful realism. At least. Stammering is the native eloquence of us fog-people.* 11

Stammering is <u>not</u> the native eloquence of the Tyrones. And it is this fact which makes *Long Day's Journey* so difficult to translate. The language that is available in modern Chinese drama will serve for submissive acceptance, for open conflict and even for regret and recrimination, but modern Chinese has few facilities for the probing of lacerated wounds, the anguish as these wounds are touched. And finally, the healing of wounds through understanding and acceptance are things difficult to enact in the dramatic language that we Chinese have at our disposal. The most dramatic and important action in *Long Day's Journey* is the stripping of masks and illusions and this is done mainly through the language. When the Tyrones drop their masks, words pour forth from them in their soliloquies and monologues. Mary's monologue at the end of Act II, for example, reveals her alienation from her family and from the realities of the world around her. Lonely and full of guilt she speaks of her longing for the life of the virginal girl she once was - as if speaking to the girl of her past could assuage the loneliness of the woman of the present.

What further complicates the problem of translating *Long Day's Journey* is that in this play O'Neill has rejected nearly all the visual and sound effects with which he experimented on stage for nearly all his life. The vision of the dramatist is communicated almost entirely through the language of the play.[12] If O'Neill's vision is to be passed over intact, the translator must rise to the task of stretching his imagination as well as extending the possibilities of his native tongue in order to find expression for the ambivalent feelings and complexities of emotions which dominate the play. These qualities are most clearly manifested in the last act of the play where they are built into a sequence of painful confessions leading to the final revelations composed in rhythms of pain and ending finally in a harrowing climax.

Structurally this final act of *Long Day's Journey* is built on two colloquies - between Tyrone and Edmund and between Edmund and Jamie - followed by a long soliloquy by Mary which concludes the act and the play. Edmund and Tyrone evoke the past only to flee from the present. Edmund's description of his family as "fog people" is apt. They are befogged by whiskey, drugs, pain, and by the past which is symbolized in the actual fog which descends on them until they are completely wrapped by it. Fogging causes them to drift in slow almost dreamlike movements - activities cease and the play becomes a play for voices. The loss, the pain and the lamentations are carried solely through the language.

Irony is the prevailing mode of the scene between Edmund and Tyrone. Irony in any language is difficult enough to capture and almost impossible to render in translation, especially when the audience for which the text is to be translated is unaccustomed to that particular use of irony. The colloquy between Edmund and his father depends almost entirely on an understanding of the use of irony as a cover for the emotions which both characters do not wish to reveal but which the audience can guess if it is used to displays of this kind of defence mechanism. Tyrone's absurd miserliness is second-nature to him and when it is ridiculed by Edmund, he is enraged and counter-attacks only to regret it as he remembers that his son is ill with the deadly consumption. He moves to an apology and touched by his gesture Edmund also apologizes and offers to switch off the light. But the minute they reveal their vulnerable feelings, both withdraw into a covering barrage of hurtful attack and sardonic baiting. The thrust and parry is merely a game to hide their real emotional feelings. But if the translator fails to put this delicate ambivalence across to his readers and audience, he comes into real danger of confusing the dramatic signals for them. They will very likely seize upon the superficial hostility of the father and son mistaking it for their real relationship. The suppleness of O'Neill's language allows the play an ambivalence of feeling - the neurotic fear of Tyrone disguised in anger at the wastage of electricity, the tentative offer of love and, at the crucial moment before it is accepted and exchanged, the fearful withdrawal of it before it is taken and exploited. But unfortunately ambiguity of feeling has not been explored to any great extent in modern Chinese drama. The translator has to extend the resources and the spectrum of language available to him to capture the full gamut of O'Neill's expressive possibilities.

Ambiguity of familial relationships is also foreign to a Chinese audience accustomed to clear cut and well-defined roles in the family. Edmund's sardonic baiting of his father might well be construed as a lack of filial piety, which is one of the most strongly guarded taboos in Chinese culture. Trying to render O'Neill's dramatization of the ambiguous relationships between each and every member of his fictional family and having to explore certain taboos in self-expression demands tact and a certainty of touch from the translator if he is not to alienate his audience before he can draw them into understanding the paradoxical relationships of the Tyrones. The complex love-hate relationship of the two brothers is, in a sense, even more difficult to capture and put over than all the other familial relationships in the play.

Loving and hating Edmund, Jamie has tried to create Edmund in his own image, possessing him in an almost demonic way. To get this across O'Neill uses the Frankenstein image: "Hell, you're more than my brother. I made you! You're my Frankenstein!" But though it is difficult enough to find an equivalent image in Chinese for Frankenstein - an image which takes in creator and destroyer - it is, I think even more difficult and crucial to convey the tone of envy, hatred, love and regret in Jamie's attitude towards Edmund. The ambiguity of these feelings is largely conveyed in the tension of the language which O'Neill gives Jamie. This is a tension between the soft lyrical terms under guise of slang and colloquiallism and the outburst of harsh feelings. This tension is, of course, reinforced by Jamie's shift between drunkenness and consciousness. Unless one is able to capture the image shifts, the tension in the language and the conflict in the heart of Jamie as he slips from drunken subconscious to lucid consciousness, one will surely lose the point of this important colloquy - that Jamie is the creator and destroyer of Edmund. By moulding Edmund's taste and encouraging him to write, Jamie gave Edmund a creative life, but almost as soon as he gave life he withdrew it by dragging Edmund down into a world of whores and alcohol and making a "bum" out of him. Was it that Jamie had corrupted young Edmund's life with sensuality? Or was it that he had provided Edmund with a creative route of escape - the route that O'Neill himself was to take?

Edmund has at least caught a glimpse of "vision of beatitude"; Jamie is condemned to live without even a hope of beatitude or of love. Like his brother and his father, he is dependent on his mother. But while their love for Mary is based on devotion and affection, Jamie's love for her is born of oedipal rejection and his need for her is the central explanation of his despair with life. Mary, as the biblical name suggests, is the source of life for the three men in her life: the two months during which Mary returned to normal, Tyrone describes as "heaven" - not only because she is there for him to love,but also because her presence draws all four of them together, overriding all the animosity in them. She is the hub around which they move, happy just to be in her presence. However, as she withdraws from them deeper and deeper into the past and into herself, the family disintegrates along with her. Her last soliloquy poetically evokes all the themes of the play. In it she re-enacts all the dreams of her youth and in doing so sums up the utter hopelessness of the entire family. She is looking for her lost faith, their lost faith, which has turned yellow with age like her wedding gown. And her desperate speech ends:

> *That was in the winter of the senior year. Then in the springtime something happened to me. Yes, I remember. I fell in love with James Tyrone and was so happy for a time.* 13

Time, the keyword of this speech and of the whole play, ends the play and all four characters' long journey into themselves. Time, which spans the years and which recapitulates the blighted hopes, the emotional ambivalence and the sense of imprisonment in the fate and guilt that the family shares, is the central symbol. The simplicity and chastity of Mary's soliloquy challenges the sensitivity of the translator of *Long Day's Journey* as he is forced to strip the usual dramatic language open to him of its usual clutter of clichés of recrimination to come up with a language pure enough to sustain this colloquy. It must be pure yet reverberative in its sound and rhythm so that as the fog and the night descend to enshroud the Tyrones, O'Neill may be seen as having transcended what has overwhelmed his characters.

> *Who wants to see life as it is, if they can help it? It's the three Gorgons in one. You look in their faces and die. Or it's Pan. You see him and die - that is, inside you - and have to go on living as a ghost.* 14

The point is that O'Neill has seen life as it is. He has not only survived to talk about it but found a new language in which to talk about his experience of "facing" his "dead".

How to grasp and communicate this new language which O'Neill has found and used in *Long Day's Journey* remains the key problem of translating this play. O'Neill expresses the subtle nuances of love and hate, recrimination and acceptance, accusation and forgiveness, as well as the ambiguities of anguish, pain, concern and finally tranquility and equanimity through the use of images (his own as well as borrowings from the wealth of European poetry and philosophy); He does this partly through his sure control over the rhythm of the language which gives ordinary speech a surcharge of passion and emotion, and most importantly through an intuitive yet disciplined ability to make his language say less and suggest more. He achieves this by exploiting the more intimate inner relationships and undertones within the language. This last and most significant achievement is the achievement of finding what Valéry perhaps means by <un language dans le language> - a language within a language.

There is very little that the translator can do to retain the plethora of meanings and significance which has grown around the images and mythology of a foreign culture. One can and must try to convey the mood and meaning of, say, Dawson's poetry as best as one can, in the hope that the local audience will understand that Edmund's prediliction for quoting it is indicative of his subconscious suicidal instincts. One is baulked by the frequent use of images like Frankenstein, Gorgon, Pan and even the Nietzschean Superman - images which carry such a wealth of emotional and philosophical connotations that, obviously, a simple transliteration of these names would only suggest a gibberish of names, if anything, to an audience with no background in European literature and philosophy. But even then one can search for equivalents in one's own culture and mythology. Failing that, one can perhaps slip in an explicatory phrase or two. But the translator feels his deepest sense of loss and his own inadequacy when he searches into the dramatic language which he has inherited from his own drama. He finds that the language available is useful only for direct, descriptive, textural communication. There does not exist a subtextural convention in modern Chinese drama for him to fall back on. This is when the translator has to teach himself to work in a much more self-conscious way towards finding a new language. He has to be critical and creative at the same time so that he can also build, layer upon layer, the complexities of the original as its subtext into his translation. In short, he has to re-evaluate his own language and then teach his audience to learn and appreciate this new language. And in this case he has to assume the function of creating a new language - a function which is usually ascribed to writers in most situations. The value of reading or watching such a play in translation is thus enormously amplified: it will not only show how a foreign language works,but it will also hopefully open up the limitations of modern Chinese dramatic language and thereby add one more dimension to modern Chinese drama. For with every attempt at pushing back the limitations of art goes the discovery of limitations beyond which it seems impossible to go.

In reassessing our own language we also reassess our culture which has developed this language. The dramatist Ts'ao Yu has earlier been cited as having come closest to finding a language which could carry the full force of the more private and ambiguous feelings, of finding a subtext for the language of modern Chinese drama. But unfortunately such attempts as he made were never developed either by himself or by those dramatists who came after him. Drama was a much neglected genre before the advent of Ts'ao Yu, and after the Yanan Forum of 1942 which nailed down the fate of literature, including drama, as being subservient to revolution no dramatist could experiment with the genre as Ts'ao Yu had left it. Thus, willy-nilly, Ts'ao Yu has attained an almost "mythic" stature in the history of modern Chinese drama. His plays have become the model for those who aspire to write in the Western dramatic form and audience responses to them have almost crystallized into a standard of expectations and demands for modern plays. And since even Ts'ao Yu ostensibly seemed to have moved in the direction of social realism, of showing a greater interest in social problems than in the exploration of private feelings, this perhaps explains why the drift of modern Chinese drama has moved in the direction of the communication of ideas rather than in the direction of revelation and sharing of existential experience. In any case, most audiences are more disposed to being confronted with new ideas than with new experiences, for, in the words of D.H. Lawrence: "The world does not fear a new idea. It can pigeonhole any new idea. But it can't pigeonhole an experience." Lawrence suggests that the world fears an experience because experience demands an active response. Possibly we have been unwilling to respond actively to an experience in literature because experiences in literature are so frightening - especially experiences in drama which are so direct and immediate. The dramatist relentlessly and mercilessly turns a painful experience on his audience as a dentist turns a drill on an aching tooth: the desire to escape from both situations is perfectly understandable. Perhaps we have also avoided awful experiences because solutions can rarely be found for them and in such cases acceptance, even blind acceptance without understanding, is considered the best of the non-solutions. This largely accounts for the popularity of realistic plays with Chinese audiences since social problems can at least be resolved by some change, no matter how difficult it may be to work for that change.

If *Long Day's Journey* was merely a documentation of one particular family's suffering for which there was no solution and no escape, then perhaps evasion might be the best course to take for an audience - certainly a Chinese audience would reject *Long Day's Journey* from sheer fright at the unrestrained revelation of lacerated feelings and the depth of pain evoked by these open wounds. But as we watch the Tyrones attack one another and comfort one another in turn in a paradox of hatred, guilt and love, we become less aware of the lacerations and pain and more aware of an unremitting movement "behind life", to borrow O'Neill's description of expressionist drama. We become aware of the movement of the play expanding inwards, towards itself, as well as outward on the action of the play. This movement "behind life" is what lifts the play out of the genre of social documentary or domestic tragedy onto a higher plane by enlarging the audience's knowledge of the suffering of the play's characters arising from the action. The powerful events of the play supercharged with probing and pain grip our attention and sympathy. But in the last analysis, we are aware not only of the pain of the Tyrones but of life itself. By the end of the play we are convinced that suffering is the only reality and understanding and acceptance the only possible attitude to take in life. Suffering in *Long Day's Journey* is made so real and powerful because it operates on two levels - on the level of fiction and on the level of actuality. And the audience is made to share in the suffering on the level of the fictional Tyrone family as well as that of the universal family - a point which Travis Bogard (1972) makes so well in his study of this play:

> *An emotion appropriate to an aesthetic experience and an emotion evoked by reality join to create in the spectators a capacity for pity that extends well beyond the boundaries of the theatre and rises to an acknowledgement of exceptional purity: that the universality of pain makes pity and understanding and forgiveness the greatest of human needs.* 15

If *Long Day's Journey* is translated and presented with the full force of the universal experience of suffering and understanding and forgiveness, no audience, not even one which has made evasion of experience an art, will be able to escape its shattering impact. No audience will be able to turn away from an active response to the experience which it engenders. This play will then succeed, if nothing else, in detaching the audience from their habits of thought and feeling which their culture has imposed on them. And it will provide them with a new ground and vantage point from which to judge and perhaps even to revise the culture which has engendered these habits. The way O'Neill finally works out his obsessions with his fictional family - in a spirit of complete honesty and without any prohibiting conventions in talk or action - should teach us to reassess our own fictional and actual experiences and obsessions of our families. Certainly it ought to show us quite clearly that response to an intolerable situation need not only be a choice between an escape from the situation in terms of flight on the one hand, or open rebellion and sullen acceptance on the other. There is a third way and the play enacts it for us. In the last resort, culture would be transcended if, by reading or watching a play in translation,one learnt to surrender oneself to experience without being chained by societal bonds, by conventional social morality or even by the limitations of the language which tie us to these societal bonds. If we can escape cultural limitations,we come close to experiencing what Arnold called "the fullness of spiritual perfection" which is the committed aim of not only the best of drama but the best of all the arts.

CHAPTER 6

Audience Aids for Non-Literary Allusions? Observations on the Transposition of Essential Technicalities in the Sea Plays of Eugene O'Neill

ERNST O. FINK

I. Even before the curtain went up in the '76/'77 Hamburg production of the *Tempest* that winter, Prospero was out there front-stage, right by the footlights, brandishing the coarse model of a three-masted sailing ship. As he was toying with it in pantomime, making that plaything of a vessel in his arms "mount up to the heaven, and go down again to the depths", thunder and lightning began to roll in from behind the curtain. With a particularly vicious thunderbolt the rigging of the model burst into flames, and Prospero flung it wide - literally casting it away into the wings as the curtain opened on the riotous efforts of the crew to save Alonso's ship about to be driven ashore on Prospero's island.

As Prospero's charade merged into a life-size shipwreck it sealed comprehension of the opening dialogues on "deck" of the foundering ship. Even the most landlubberly among the audience couldn't help being 'with it' from the beginning; and the few who might have harboured qualms about withered naturalism would have felt reassured by their early insight into the nature of the "direful spectacle of the wreck" as artifice. The pre-'view' by blazing eyeful anticipated Prospero's naval powers as reviewed by Miranda in the next scene with woeful words. Evidently the Hamburg audience were being treated to a gratuitous visualization - in fact they were prodded into acceptance of a dated stock opening. The non-verbal expository scene of the Hamburg *Tempest* suggests that even in a port town with a long seafaring tradition, the modern producer would prefer to rely on standing non-verbal conventions rather than to trust his audience with the transposition of historical technicalities in nautical language.

For obvious reasons the audience's alienation from historical technology is more evident in the field of drama than in other literary genres, and it is even more obvious in the plays of modern writers. But the sprouting of land-based radar and the development of automated radar guidance has made the fog-horn in Eugene O'Neill's *Long Day's Journey Into Night* an anachronism in northern waters in our lifetime. From this point of view we propose to take a close look at the producer's chances with O'Neill's *Seven Plays of the Sea.* [1]

II. In his sea plays, O'Neill's quest for a new "Language of the Theatre" [2] reveals itself in a wide range of attempts to express the full scope of his subject. This includes the voices of the men who actually worked on the ships, both in the job and out of the job or "on the beach", as O'Neill himself used to put it. It further includes the "voices" of things that speak out for what the men (and women) have gone through, or what is going on around them when the audience is intent on the dialogue alone. For example, "oilskins and sou' wester glistening with drops of water" spell out 'fog' eloquently when Yank is about to ship on his last voyage. Finally it includes nature - directly or indirectly, soft-spoken or resounding, at times vociferous far beyond the speech of the cast.

Nature was perhaps most fittingly illustrated in one of the performances of O'Neill's play *Bound East for Cardiff* at the Provincetown Wharf Theatre. Susan Glaspell recalled this performance:

> *'The sea has been good to O'Neill,' she would write. 'It was there for his opening. There was a fog, just as the script demanded, fog bell in the harbor. The tide was in, and it washed under us and around, spraying through the holes in the floor, giving us the rhythm and the flavour of the sea while the big dying sailor talked to his friend Drisc of the life he had always wanted deep in the land, where you'd never see a ship or smell the sea.' When it was all over, 'the old wharf,' Susan Glaspell said, 'shook with applause.'* [3]

Later tradition must have invested the play with even more meaning, for, when it was recently revived for academic purposes at Hamburg University, the sea under the flooring planks of the playhouse had become the "ground swell". This is one of the most persistent voices of the sea in T.S. Eliot's *Four Quartets*, the one that "is and was from the beginning" (Dry Salvages I), the time keeper of Eternity. Although we are not concerned with the obvious exaltation expressed by Eliot, it is certainly not out of line with O'Neill's view of the sea as an embodiment of eternity. We would like to consider it to be an example of response to the far-flung appeal "voiced" by the sea plays outside the script.

The example given of the "ground swell" indicates that much of O'Neill's language of the sea retains its appeal and is not affected by modern jargon. Nature still exercises much of her old spell. However, it is different with the language expressed by things. As we intimated above with regard to the fog horn in *Long Day's Journey Into Night,* a struggle for survival is on in the field of technical language in the narrower sense of the word; wherever it was used as an objective correlative in O'Neill's day, it will have to be gauged anew as to whether it still relates to anything outside the maritime museums - or whether, to put it bluntly, *'Ile* can reasonably be staged only in the hold of the "Charles W. Morgan" at Mystic Seaport, Connecticut, where the old whaling ship lingers in her berth of concrete ... The vast changes in the nature of most "things" in seafaring since the end of World War II, have altered the "objectivity" of many things that were useful correlatives before. Between building and scrapping, the changes wrought by technological development, by the laws of "profit and loss", and last but not least by the seamen's unions, have already done away with so much in the outward appearance of things as they were in O'Neill's day, that many a young spectator may find the cramped quarters in the fo'c'sle of the *S.S. Glencairn* just so much overdue social awareness. Of course there are still those large pockets of back-lag, particularly among the fleets of the flags "of convenience", where Glencairn conditions could be called genuinely realistic even today. However, they are being inexorably removed, to be replaced by mechanized cargo handling, navigational aids, and a measure of protection for the sailor in foreign ports of which the old hand "before the mast" could never have dreamt. This portion of the language in the sea plays therefore stands most in danger of becoming "archaic". Since it is largely obsolete, it would require a conscientiously historical setting to be staged without a disconcerting time-lag between things as the play would have them be, and as the audience know them to be. However, the major portion of the text of each of these plays consists of human speech - neither the language of things nor of atmosphere, but simply the utterances of human beings trying to communicate.

It is here that the language of the sea plays dons its greatest variety in vocabulary, texture, and articulation. Between blasphemy and benediction it comprises a great deal of down-to-earth colloquial language, much of which cannot be called sea language in the strict sense of the word, and none of which aspires to be "technical navigation" in the terms of Johnson vs. Dryden. It is rich in texture - it withstands analysis for quite some time before losing its "juiciness", and will "cling" to a character even when it is broken down for close scrutiny. O'Neill's characters remain articulate at all times between ecstasy and agony - Captain Bartlett does greet the drowned crew when at last his ship comes home, Smitty speaks out defiantly until he is gagged, and Mrs. Keeney's last words ask the very question which is the pivot of the plot.

There is biographical evidence galore of O'Neill's repertory, how he came by it, and how he made use of it. He could be "foul-mouthed", and "swear like a sailor when talking to his fellow students" in Professor Baker's 47 Workshop at Harvard.[4] And he could rise with the pipe-dreams of the more tender-hearted among his crews to a gossamer-like filigree of reminiscences, of hopes and disappointments, interwoven with the twilight of the years and the strains of music from the near-by shore, as in *The Moon of the Caribbees*. The "verbalized soul", as the scholarly categorization runs, becomes audible in "thought asides" which in their syntactic peculiarities are held to "approach the techniques of stream-of-consciousness novels".[5] As such they lend themselves perhaps more easily to translation than to transposition, but there is little need of the latter in the first place: "soul" is rarely as dated as "mind", and even less so than "matter"; therefore the language of the text seems not so much in need of audience aid for transposition as does the language of "things".

III. As we proceed to examine that portion of O'Neill's language of the theatre which may properly, if provisionally, be termed a language of "things", it becomes necessary to substantiate the situational context of the plays. Of those under scrutiny here, four were first brought together into a unified framework in 1924, when *The Moon of the Caribbees*, *The Long Voyage Home*, *In the Zone*, and *Bound East for Cardiff* were staged as a cycle by Frank Shay's Barnstormers of Provincetown under the title *S.S. Glencairn*. Even a brief comparison of *dramatis personae* reveals continuation of a number of characters at least by name through the four of them. In fact "the identity of the crew goes through the series and welds the four one-acts into a long play", as O'Neill himself said in an interview.[6] The other three in the current edition mentioned above, can hardly be considered to belong with them. *The Rope* is entirely out of place; in this tryst of hate on the farm, the sea serves only as a receptacle to $20 gold coins playfully squandered by a slow-witted child. Any deep water hole or river running by would have done better. The other two, *'Ile* and *Where the Cross Is Made* are genuine "plays of the sea"; yet they stand apart from the Glencairn plays for a number of reasons: their cast is not identical with any of the Glencairn casts, their setting perceptibly antedates the Glencairn settings, and they are both much more protagonist-centred. However, they share in what O'Neill so aptly called the "spirit of the sea", and in this respect will allow us to set off the characteristics of the *S.S. Glencairn* plays that much more distinctly.

There is no hierarchy or rank to help with the remainder; neither does external evidence by date of composition, of production, or by arrangement in the extant edition imply any form of sequence. Therefore, it seems legitimate that in our concern with the language of "things", we rely on internal evidence for the order in which to consider them.

In the Zone presents the most recent setting of the six, pin-pointed like none of the rest in "the fall of the year 1915". The British tramp steamer "Glencairn" is about to enter the "war zone", that area of the Atlantic to the west of the British Isles where submarines of the Imperial German Navy might be lying in wait to torpedo her without warning. She is carrying ammunitions - and those were the days before the convoy system was imposed ... The crew are understandably tense as these circumstances are articulated when close on midnight (Eight Bells!) the new watch gets ready. Smitty's overprotective care of his love letters has not escaped detection by the wary crew - high-strung, they take him for a spy and pillory him while trying to get at the suspected "code" in his letters. The latest of these, seven months old, gives him away - not as a spy, but as a jilted lover. As he winces under their reading out his deepest secrets, recognition of their over-doing the spyhunt dawns on them. A withered flower from one of the letters drops to the floor and clinches insight and shame. They have all visibly entered the "war zone" ...

Technically, the play pivots on the enforced intimacy of the "Glencairn" fo'c'sle. It is certainly closer to sailing ship accommodation than to today's quarters which would allow Smitty a great deal more privacy. The dried-up flower is part of what O'Neill himself criticized as "theatrical sentimentalism" in this play. [7] And this final touch is not relieved, as in *The Long Voyage Home*, by any twist of irony on the part of Driscoll.

Bound East for Cardiff gets those "bleedin' horficers" in who are purposely left out of the war zone "inquest". It is the forecastle of the "Glencairn" again, and it is peace time, but Death is aboard: Yank is dying in his bunk of internal injuries, which he suffered when he fell from a ladder in the hold. The Captain and the Second Mate are about for some time, but they are quite helpless - evidently the play has its setting date from a time when nautical officers were not yet required to extend their medical care into the field of diagnosis. They are more compassionate, to be sure, but not much more capable, than Smollett's surgeons. As Yank lies dying, this "Everyman of the Sea" has the audience share in his great summing-up which with all its simplicity strikes a good many chords that have been turned into themes elsewhere by O'Neill, as well as by Masefield, by Conrad, by Kipling, to name only the most prominent here. Almost without exception, however, the themes take us back into sailing ship days - and so his ultimate worry is indeed to be buried at sea. Today he would have been whisked off to sickbay at once, and with seven days out from Cardiff he wouldn't have a chance of being "committed to the deep". Then again, he might not be half as keen on getting buried on dry land these days - not to mention the notion of a resting place in consecrated ground. Yank's final encounter with the "pretty lady dressed in black" seals his passing in terms of a somewhat facile allegory, which, however, serves well to balance the heavy sign of "The fog's lifted".

The Moon of the Caribbees, O'Neill's first play with music, owes a good deal of its intriguing atmosphere to the ingredients of the proverbial sailors' idea of the Blessed Isles, "where crews is always layin' aft for double-tots o' rum / 'N' there's dancin' 'n' fiddlin' of ev'ry kind o' sort" as the *Salt Water Ballads* would have it.[8] The men on board the "Glencairn" are out to have a good time; being denied their shore-leave, they get the bumboat girls to smuggle rum when they come on board for the night. Intoxication is only to be had "wid the wimin", and the balmy night is all in their favour, but as the party gets out of hand the outsider Smitty saves himself from his haunting memories by joining the "bunch" in the forecastle off-stage. As the strains of the music from the palm-fringed shore re-establish themselves, "the mood of the moonlight (is) made audible". - The setting hovers half-way between tramp-ship leisure and travel poster gaiety. What little action there is, is triggered by the captain's order not to bring any alcohol on board. In the a.m. letter to Clark, O'Neill put Smitty in his place with respect to "the sea's truth":

> *Smitty in the stuffy, grease-paint atmosphere of* In the Zone *is magnified into a hero who attracts our sentimental sympathy. In* The Moon, *posed against a background of that beauty, sad because it is eternal, which is one of the revealing moods of the sea's truth, his silhouetted gestures of self-pity, are reduced to their proper insignificance, his thin whine of weakness is lost in the silence which it was mean enough to disturb, we get the perspective to judge him - and the others - and we find his sentimental posing much more out of harmony with truth, much less in tune with beauty, than the honest vulgarity of his mates.* [9]

One wonders whether Smitty's talking "mem'ries" outweighs his drinking sufficiently to warrant O'Neill's indictment. In the eyes of the audience Smitty's steadfast hold on the bottle may well compete in its visual significance with the linguistic significance of his recurrent "whine of weakness". His refusal to make free with Pearl does not constitute an unequivocal visual sign either, as a number of the rest of the crew are resolved to do without female company, too. The transposition of Smitty's character seems to vacillate between mutually exclusive signs.

The Long Voyage Home takes the audience farther back into the age of transition from wind-ships to steamers. Four of the "Glencairn" crew have been paid off in London and are expected to hit a waterfront dive where the proprietor and his crimping helper plan to shanghai one of them for a full-rigger bound around Cape Horn. The nobly naive Swede Olson is done in eventually, in spite of his valiant efforts not to touch liquor any more - he wants so badly to get home, see his old mother, and take up farming with the help of his savings. He is quite the noble sailor out on "Hell's Pavement", and O'Neill preys on the feelings of the audience when he has them visualize the trap to be sprung:

> *Bloody windjammer - skys'l yarder - full rigged - painted white - been layin' at the dock above 'ere fur a month ... The capt'n says as 'e wants a man special bad - ter-night. They sails at daybreak termorrer ... The capt'n an' mate are bloody slave-drivers, an' they're bound down round the 'Orn. They 'arf starved the 'ands on the last trip 'ere, an' no one'll dare ship on 'er ...*[10]

The sailing ship becomes Doom incarnate, and Fate is dead set against poor Olson. The play is saved from sheer melodrama by Driscoll taking Olson's disappearance as a sure sign of well-being: "Who'd think Ollie'd be sich a divil wid the wimin? ..." The long voyage home is far from over.

'Ile and *Where the Cross Is Made* stand apart from the four hitherto mentioned, in that they are not based on the "Glencairn" crew and derive their setting altogether from earlier times. For *'Ile* it is the steam whaler "Atlantic Queen", ice-bound in northern waters in her second year out, with only "a measly four hundred barrel of ile" to show for it. The year is 1895, and the heyday of Nantucket and New Bedford whaling is over. The steam whaler as such, by itself a dead end in shipping history, conveys something of the determination of Death Larsen and his hunters to keep an established trade profitable beyond its day. In *'Ile* the skipper is at last prevailed upon by his near-mutinous crew and his wife to give up the futile wait, when suddenly the ice does break up and clear a passage "to no'th'ard" and to whales blowing. He cannot resist this temptation to "git the ile", but as he is having the boats lowered his wife goes insane: the solitary confinement of the northern seas which severely taxed the endurance and loyalty of the crew, has broken hers.

Greed is made to come out as a major impetus in the other play, too; but it takes on a fairytale ambiguity in *Where the Cross Is Made*. Old Captain

Isaiah Bartlett has been waiting three years for his ship to return - the schooner "Mary Allen" which he fitted out at the cost of mortgaging his home, to bring back the treasure he discovered when ship-wrecked years before. The "Mary Allen" will never come home, though, for she was sighted bottom up after a hurricane in the Celebes Sea. Bartlett knows, his son and his daughter know, but Bartlett won't believe. From the upper part of his home, which he turned into cabin and poop-deck of a sailing ship, he keeps a nightly lookout for "a red and a green light at the mainmast-head" - the signal agreed upon with his three fellow-survivors for when they would be coming with the treasure recovered from "where the cross is made" in their map of shipwreck days. So far it is staple diet for adventure stories; but modern-day exigencies zero in on old Bartlett - the mortgage is to be foreclosed, and he is to be taken to an asylum. The very night the doctor comes by to acquaint himself with the situation of the "lunatic", the "Mary Allen" makes port and the treasure is brought to Bartlett: "The sound of the wind and sea suddenly ceases ... A dense green glow floods slowly in rhythmic waves like a liquid into the room - as of great depths of the sea faintly penetrated by light", and the "forms" of the three fellow treasure-hunters "glide silently into the room", evidently drowned - but home at last with the chests. Bartlett dies peacefully, but in front of a dazed audience the spell is lodged anew in young Bartlett.

Our review of the situational context of the sea plays will have borne out the importance of the "say" things have had in O'Neill's settings. They constitute a fairly comprehensive array of "stations" in an A.B. seaman's universe of O'Neill's day, and are presented within an historically definable framework. Materially, the forecastle substantiates confinement as a recurrent theme. It is mostly collective confinement, sometimes by way of pillory, cage, threat, or unfulfilled promise of escape. In *'Ile* the ice barriers assume confining functions for the crew *and* the quarterdeck. For old Captain Bartlett the end of the belief in his ship is forced by reality closing in on him in terms of his creditor and the asylum. Again, his make-believe quarters on shore, a veritable stage-on-the-stage, provide the props for his life-sustaining dream. This is the rub: the forecastle, for all its confinement, is never only cage, but also strong-hold for the men, truly a "castle" providing bedrock for their identity: the porthole accidentally left unclosed triggers suspicion as if it was a breach in the wall (*Zone*); to the dying Yank the fo'c'sle serves at least as long as it keeps the fog out (*Cardiff*); it is a true retreat, out of earshot of the bridge, and it is good to rejoin the "bunch" even for the outsider Smitty (*Caribbees*); and Olson in his abortive "sortie" is lost once his fellow fo'c'sle mates leave him (*Voyage*). There is no need to go into details about the role of the fog here, as it is sufficiently set out elsewhere, and speaks a more "atmospheric" language anyway. Considering, however, the pains O'Neill has taken to ensure that the language of the text would get across - he actually translates every daytime indication from "bells" into hours on the clock, avoids technical terms, and reproduces in writing what may be all too outlandish in pronunciation like "from Bewnezerry (Buenos Aires)" - we will now proceed to weigh the possibilities of how to ensure acceptance of his language of "things" with latterday audiences.

IV. On the whole, then, it is not so much the language of the text which may fail to reach the addressee in the audience as, much rather, that of "things". Or to put it in a variant of Conrad's famous saying, in O'Neill's sea plays there is "nothing wrong with the men, it's the ships in them..." It is the "S.S. Glencairn" in particular which is tainted by her being so dated. The "Mary Allen", the "Amindra", and even Captain Keeney's steam whaler belong to a period of our seafaring past which is historically closed. These ships live on as part of our maritime heritage which by its very remoteness has rendered them immovable, no longer "subject to change". But the "Glencairn" belonged to the present at the time of the composition of these plays; she was contemporary with O'Neill, and in many ways typical of her day. She remained so until the advent of the super tanker, of the ULC's, and of containerization. Today she is dated as the immediate forerunner of these recent developments, and her datedness conveys upon her a tinge of "sawdust realism" - the very thing her creator has always despised.

Theoretically there are two ways in which to remedy this. The "Glencairn" as a stage might be brought up to date by modernizing her - bringing her "properties" in line with conditions on board, say, "Australian Enterprise", "Melbourne Express", or "Columbus Australia". This would preserve her as a contemporary cargo carrier and allow for a considerable amount of identification by any A.B. seaman who chanced to find himself in the auditorium. Surely this would be in keeping with her character, as the name of the ship implies - as typical a name for a type of ship as ever there was, to any one at all familiar with names in the heyday of British shipping, even without going into the annals of the British Glen Line. It would entail, however, an impossible amount of inconsistency in plot, as we have suggested above (III) in basing our outlines of the plays on technical detail of the historical settings. Therefore the practical way to go would be in the other direction, i.e. to enhance the "Glencairn" of O'Neill's days by making her the "absolute ship", a sort of Flying Dutchman under steam. If she could be delivered of her period trappings, she might become more meaningful. If ways could be found to retain her as a stage without relying on her open-air-museum qualities, she might become something of a timeless vessel for Man's predicament ...

We shall not pretend in this paper to have final solutions up the sleeve. But given a philologist's respect for the author's text as script, and given our findings that much of the sea plays' datedness stems from their "dated stage" of *S.S. Glencairn*, we would suggest tentatively to divest the text of some of its more evident "technicality" to be re-created *before* the curtain. To bring out technical aspects of a given play somewhere closer to the audience than the action of the script proper, may result in the dissociation of the two; it will, however, surely allow the text to go unfettered and to hold the stage unrivalled. At the same time the audience is exposed to the full impact of the technology involved in having the visual aspects of it literally before their eyes - closer than by way of backdrops, and with a full new range of stressing it at the discretion of the producer ... For example, we would begin by pointing out the as yet widely unused surface of the curtain. Even before the beginning of the play the curtain might serve as a giant still to combine the dramatic headlines of U-boat warfare - the very hopes and fears which must have been uppermost in the minds of the men about to enter the "Zone". DosPassos' newsreel technique might be employed to bring home to the audience the hectic headlines of 1915, the year of the sinking of the "Lusitania" ... For both *In the Zone* and *Bound East for Cardiff* a certain degree of timelessness might be achieved for the stage by having the interior of the ship modelled along the lines of the first scene in *The Hairy Ape*, with "bright steel" forming a cage-like framework. O'Neill is said to have left perhaps "too much to the director and the stage-carpenter",[11] so we will suggest to supply the deficiency by first drawing on the rest of his plays, as this seems the most legitimate interpolation imaginable. The "pretty lady dressed in black" who comes to fetch Yank might enter his quarters from the auditorium as a palpable member of the cast, invisible only to the rest of the crew - and with just a bit of screen effects trickery she might even come aboard just as the "fog" lifts ... Screen effects could also be employed to have the audience visualize something of the lotus eater atmosphere in *The Moon of the Caribbees* by putting together the palm-fringed "coral beach, white in the moonlight" with the anchorage of Masefield's "Port of Many Ships" and adding perhaps a touch of Gauguin's Tahiti ... - but again, not as a back-drop, but right in front of the audience for them to hold on to visually whenever they are not occupied with the spoken word on the "Glencairn's" main deck. The defeat of Olson's new-life resolutions could be accompanied by having the contending futures of the little farm in Sweden and the Horn-bound full-rigger to the right and left of the stage, appearing and disappearing with varied lighting, much like Marlowe's good and bad angels at odds about Faustus ... For *'Ile*, Mrs. Keeney's piano should be heard, soft-spoken, before the curtain opens - it would counterpoint the mad finale; and for what Keeney himself sees to "no'th'ard" all the time, either reconnaissance plane pictures of Arctic wastes or Gustave Doré's illustrations for Coleridge's *Ancient Mariner* would allow the audience to share his "view" ... And for *Where the Cross Is Made*, some sort of over-size treasure map for the auditorium to see is a must, cross or no cross; it is even more important, however, to have a veritable masthead way out in front of the action, with lamps which light up red over green for the audience when Bartlett "sees" his ship come home ...

V. There is no playwright to match O'Neill as a shipwright. He mans his stage with real sailors, and he has a lot of ship on stage, and most of it is steamer. Three voices can be distinguished in the language of his plays: the voices of the men, of Nature, and of things. The first two are transcribed closely by the text, the last loosely by stage directions and plot. We have refrained from tampering with the text. It is singularly devoid of nautical language, and we must respect the "inarticulate nobility" of O'Neill's crews. There really is no character among them to compare with Shakespeare's bosun. But a number of "things" have a lot to say that may require attention to transposition today - technicalities ranging from the porthole accidentally left open to fancy steamerlights for a missing schooner. As long as the context was contemporary to both author and audience, such things would come across at face value, whether acoustic or visual. For today's audiences, however, existing conventions will in due course prove increasingly unreliable. There arises the need for a re-evaluation of the expressive capacities of the signs employed. A review of the respective dependence of the plays has led us to suggest reinforcement by stage carpentry, by lighting, by screen effects "audience-wards" from the stage proper. "Before the curtain" may have to become the keyword for both time and place of such "situational footnotes". Prospero's Hamburg pantomime was an outstanding example.

Transposition for today's English-speaking audiences may be just as demanding as translation into a foreign language. With "Glencairn" and "Mary Allen" the ingrained trinity of text, type, and tone defies translation. Studies of O'Neill's nomenclature have repeatedly bypassed the names of his ships.[12] Tomorrow's stage director casting about for ways and means of transposition, may find reassurance in the avowedly autobiographical and antiromantic traits of the sea plays.[13] From his early days O'Neill sympathized with goners and bygones. Later he "transposed" early days by the nostalgic props in his two make-believe homes on the ocean. "Things" would speak to him evidently much in the way they did to old Bartlett.[14] Today such properties are treasure-trove to any stage-director who seeks new ways of making his audience look and listen.

CHAPTER 7

Hazards of Adaptation: Anouilh's *Antigone* in English

IAN REID

I. Any translator of any play is likely to consider at some point the possibility of departing from a strictly faithful rendering of his original text in order to clarify certain issues for its second-hand audiences and readers. Some liberties in phrasing may of course be virtually inevitable and perfectly innocuous. But when the "translation" goes beyond those simple adjustments to make substantial excisions or additions it has become in fact an adaptation - which is capable of distorting the essential conception. In such cases, it is not pedantic to express a concern for textual propriety. Translators and producers alike need to be responsibly aware that tinkering with the surface of a text - however well-intentioned the alterations may be - can have profound consequences.

My interest in this problem dates back to my student days in New Zealand, when I had a confused correspondence with the editor of the *New Zealand Listener* about a production of Anouilh's *Antigone* broadcast by the NZBC. The program in the *Listener* had described this as "*Antigone*, by Jean Anouilh, translated by Lewis Galantière, adapted and produced by William Austin (NZBC)". Knowing the French text and the respectable Galantière translation, I listened to this broadcast - and was startled to find that some important speeches were cut and other speeches invented with no basis in either Anouilh's text or Galantière's translation. This, I presumed, must have been the producer's responsibility, since the program said he had "adapted" the play. I wrote to the *Listener* protesting that Anouilh's play had been seriously marred by Mr. Austin's decision to "delete many significant passages from the original text and interpolate several gratuitous lines of exegetical commentary". I added: "No blame can be laid at the door of Lewis Galantière, whose sympathetic translation was the ostensible basis for the radio version."

The editor retorted crisply:

> *Galantière's "sympathetic translation" was not the basis for the radio version: it was the radio version. No "significant passages" were deleted; the only interpolations were a few words to clarify visual action; and the reference to Creon as a "tyrant" was a chorus line taken verbatim from the original - from Anouilh himself.*

But my undergraduate zeal could not so easily be stifled. I answered in more detail, specifying changes that I deemed detrimental to the play's whole effect, such as the omission of what, I claimed,

> *was perhaps the crucial speech of the original play - Antigone's confession that her sacrifice is personal and pointless. When Creon asks her why she is dying, she replies (in Galantière's translation): "For nobody. For myself."*

As for the portrayal of Creon as a tyrant (in the sense of "unjust oppressor," rather than the ancient neutral meaning of "sovereign ruler"), I said I had searched Anouilh's play and Galantière's translation without finding any such reference. Would the editor care to cite one?

He was able to cite several; and he also declared that the "crucial speech" which I had cited did not appear in "Galantière's translation *as used in the first production in New York in 1946*". There, in the words I have italicized, lay the accidental explanation for our disagreement. The Galantière translation which I had been consulting - and which indeed is widely known, often reprinted - was one used in the first London production of 1949. Evidently, then, there were two versions by Galantière, one faithful and the other much less so.

Was this much ado about nothing? I think not. In what follows, I shall point out exactly how the versions differ, and how the freer adaptation led not just one New Zealand editor (and doubtless many radio listeners) but also at least some American theatre-goers to misconstrue the play's main theme. Differences between the versions are largely confined to a few passages, but these are of quite central importance. There is no need here for a sentence-by-sentence juxtaposition of each divergent section with its counterpart. Brief commentary on a handful of key speeches will suffice to demonstrate what the adaptations signify.

But first, the bibliographical facts should be detailed. For although we are concerned primarily with a comparison between 1946 and 1949 versions, the matter is slightly more complicated than that: the earlier (American) text actually appeared under two imprints, which are not quite identical. Each purports to be the adaptation used in "the first performance of *Antigone* as produced at the Cort Theatre, New York, February ... 1946, with Katharine Cornell and Cedric Hardwicke," although the text published by Random House (New York, 1946) gives the production date as February 18th (which was indeed the first night) whereas the text published by Samuel French (New York, 1947) gives it as February 19th. Whether the occasional discrepancies between these texts do reflect changes made immediately after the opening performance, or (as seems more likely) simply indicate that Galantière silently altered one of them before publication, it is now difficult - and unimportant - to decide. For the most part, they will be regarded together as variants of "the 1946 version," since the differences between them are on the whole much less extensive and significant than the differences which separate them both, on the one hand, from "the 1949 version," as I shall call it, on the other. This latter, used for the Old Vic production (February 1949) with Laurence Olivier and Vivien Leigh, was published by Methuen in 1951, and has since been gathered into Volume 2 of *Jean Anouilh: The Collected Plays*, issued by the same publisher in 1967.

II. Those among the audience who do not already know the classical story of *Antigone* when the curtain rises on Anouilh's play are soon supplied with the background information. In an expository prologue, the Chorus introduces us to each of the characters and tells us about the civil war which culminated in the deaths of Antigone's brothers, Eteocles and Polynices. Before the action begins on stage, we learn that Creon, the king, has ordered that Polynices be left to rot unburied outside the city walls; and we know that Creon's niece Antigone will defy the edict. Consequently all our attention is focused on the nature of the conflict between these two, and the terms in which they are portrayed for us in the Chorus's long opening speech are of great importance in shaping our sympathies. Yet it is right here at the very outset that the 1946 version makes some of its most drastic departures from the French source.

The Chorus begins by talking about Antigone herself, emphasizing her fatalistic sense that she must fulfil a role allotted to her:

> *Elle pense. Elle pense qu'elle va être Antigone tout à l' heure ....*
> *Elle pense qu'elle va mourir, qu'elle est jeune et qu'elle aussi, elle aurait bien aimé vivre. Mais il n'y a rien à faire. Elle s'appelle Antigone et il va falloir qu'elle joue son rôle jusqu'au bout.*

In his 1949 version Galantière rendered this accurately (" ... When your name is Antigone, there is only one part you can play; and she will have to play hers through to the end."). But in 1946 he chose to substitute for that last sentence a misleading gloss:

> *When you are on the side of the gods against the tyrant, of Man against the State, of purity against corruption - when, in short, your name is Antigone, there is only one part you can play; and she will have to play hers through to the end.*

A little further on in his exposition the Chorus turns to Creon. Anouilh's own account of the king's character is a sympathetic one; Creon is a man who reluctantly set aside his quiet personal preoccupations, his love of music, books, and antique *objects d'art* to shoulder the burden of kingship after the deaths of Oedipus, Eteocles and Polynices. And that is properly preserved in Galantière's 1949 version:

> *Creon had to roll up his sleeves and take over the kingdom. Now and then, when he goes to bed weary with the day's work, he wonders whether this business of being a leader of men is worth the trouble. But when he wakes up the problems are there to be solved; and like a conscientious workman, he does his job.*

But the 1946 version replaces those lines with a very different portrait by Galantière himself, one which falsifies the play's fundamental meaning:

> *I'll tell you something about Creon. He has a tendency to fool himself. This leader of men, this brilliant debator and logician, likes to believe that if it were not for his sense of responsibility he would step right down from the throne and go back to collecting manuscripts. But the fact is, he loves being king. He's an artist who has always believed that* he *could govern just as well as any man of action could; and he's quite sure that no god nor any man can tell* him *anything about what is best for the common people.*

This travesty of Anouilh's conception of Creon, combined with the earlier interpolation about Antigone, puts the play badly out of focus before the stage action has even got under way. We have been presented *a priori* with a supposedly definitive view of protagonist and antagonist - and it is a crudely distorted view. As the prologue of the Chorus concludes, there is another instance of this irresponsible kind of "adaptation": in lieu of the lines which the 1949 version quite rightly translates as "Now Thebes is at peace and Creon is King" we are told in the 1946 version: "And now Creon is King. A reign of terror has begun."

The next appearance of the Chorus follows scenes in which we learn that Antigone has managed to bury the body of Polynices. Her arrest by the guards and her confrontation with the King are imminent. The speech of the Chorus at this point would seem to offer little opportunity for adaptation, since it is a generalized discourse on the nature of tragedy as Anouilh sees it: as the unfolding of a wholly inevitable sequence of actions. But since Galantière has decided to impose another emphasis on the action, he deletes in his 1946 version the most central statement of that discourse: "There is a sort of fellow-feeling among characters in a tragedy: he who kills is as innocent as he who gets killed: it's all a matter of what part you are playing." [1] To have retained that sentence would have meant to contradict what Galantière's changes elsewhere signified - a black-and-white opposition between corruption and conscience, between cruel expediency and moral integrity.

The long ensuing debate between Creon and Antigone is the thematic core of the play. Theatrically, it has great impact; both characters deliver speeches of impassioned eloquence, and the balance of rhetorical power shifts to and fro several times. The most intense moment comes after Creon has reminded Antigone of the transparently silly mumbo-jumbo of the priests who conduct religious burial. She agrees that it is a shameful ritual. Here is the climax of their exchange (1949 version):

> CREON: *And you still insist upon being put to death -merely because I refuse to let your brother go out without that grotesque passport .... The whole thing is absurd!*
>
> ANTIGONE: *Yes, it's absurd.*
>
> CREON: *Then why, Antigone. Why? For whose sake? For the sake of them that believe in it? To raise them against me?*
>
> ANTIGONE: *No.*
>
> CREON: *For whom, then, if not for them and not for Polynices either?*
>
> ANTIGONE: *For nobody. For myself.*

Her position is absolute, and its stark revelation in these lines is of absolute importance for our understanding of the tragedy. Yet none of what has just been quoted appears in the 1946 version. Instead we are given a concocted substitute; when Creon asks Antigone whether she too has not been disgusted by priestly formulas (the question which in Anouilh's text she answers affirmatively), she is made by Galantière to reply:

> *No, Creon. There is God and there are His priests. And they are not the same thing. You are not free to do with men as you wish - not even when they are dead.*

CREON: *And you are going to <u>stop</u> me, are you?*

ANTIGONE: *Yes, I am going to stop you.*

Not only does this substitution weaken the dramatic effect considerably it almost inverts Antigone's stance. In Anouilh's conception, her protest at what Creon represents is made on the grounds that one *ought* to be free to act as one wishes and that *his* hands are tied. It is not the pious gesture that Galantière would have it be, but an act of naked, wilful self-assertion.

Of course Antigone does earnestly wish to bury her brother. But as the rhythms of her argument with Creon swell to their climax, it becomes increasingly clear - to us, and eventually to her - that the fundamental source of her defiance is not any sense of a social or religious principle but an instinctive revulsion from the normal demands of adult living. Many details of dialogue show that she clings throughout the action to the simplicities of childhood, to an ideal of pure innocence which cannot brook any form of compromise. At the scene's emotional peak Creon brings her to see that there is no moral basis for her stand; Polynices and Eteocles, he reveals, were both despicably disloyal to their family and their state, and Antigone's gesture is pointless. Now it is perfectly plain in Anouilh's text (and in the 1949 translation) that at this juncture Antigone, nonplussed, yields to Creon's cogency. After Creon has related how her two brothers were nothing more than "a pair of blackguards," there is "a long silence," according to the stage direction, before Antigone says ("in a mild voice"):

Why do you tell me all this?

CREON: *Would it have been better to let you die a victim to that obscene story?*

ANTIGONE: *It might have been. I had my faith.*

CREON: *What are you going to do now?*

ANTIGONE: (rises to her feet in a daze):
I shall go up to my room.

CREON: *Don't stay alone. Go and find Haemon.*
And get married quickly.

ANTIGONE: (in a whisper): *Yes.*

All that dialogue is omitted in the 1946 version, which leaps ahead to Antigone's recovery of her resoluteness. In so doing, it suppresses the significance of her death - which *should* be seen as a gratuitous act of self-destruction by which she avoids emerging from childhood sureties:

> *Moi, je veux tout, tout de suite, - et que ce soit entier, - ou alors je refuse! ... Je veux être sûre de tout aujourd'hui et que cela soit aussi beau que quand j'étais petite - ou mourir.*

Again, the 1946 version leaves out this declaration, inserting in its place an attack by Antigone on the "smugness" and "lying," of a "power-loving" Creon who "desecrates the dead." It is a fierce indictment - but of Galantière's Creon, not Anouilh's.

III. Other passages might be quoted, but they would merely underline what has been demonstrated. The question remains, however: how much does all this matter? In selecting certain discrepant areas of the Galantière material, have I exaggerated the general difference between his 1946 adaptation and his 1949 translation?

It is impossible to measure precisely the influence, beneficial or harmful, of this or that text. But if further evidence is needed to show that Galantière's two versions result in markedly different dramatic effects, that evidence lies in the fact that whereas reviewers of the London production, based faithfully on the proper text, were in no doubt of Anouilh's central themes, the American reviewers three years earlier expressed the same serious misconceptions about the true nature of the tragedy as those which the same adapted text engendered long afterwards in New Zealand. I shall illustrate this briefly.

Joseph Wood Krutch, theatre critic for *The Nation*, was by no means obtuse in his remarks on the New York production, but was nevertheless misled by the textual liberties which have been indicated above into seeing the play as centering on a conflict between the icy arguments of "a rationalizing fascist dictator" and Antigone's impassioned "conviction that necessity, the tyrant's plea, is never superior to the claims of fundamental human decency."[2] And Stark Young, writing for *New Republic*, similarly described Antigone as motivated by "respect for human instincts" and as opposed by Creon's dictatorial "malignity."[3] How, indeed, could they have seen the play otherwise, unless they had gone beyond the 1946 adaptation to examine Anouilh's play? On the other hand, English reviewers had the great advantage of seeing a production that registered the subtleties of the French original; accordingly they were able to recognize clearly what was at issue in the confrontation between the king and his niece. The commentary by Worsley in *The New Statesman and Nation* is representative enough to suffice for quotation.[4] Anouilh's *Antigone*, says Worsley,

> *does not embody the heroic courage of the individual hurling herself against implacable power and invoking, as she goes to her doom, the great terms of vindication, Justice, Conscience, The Moral Law. This Antigone is a small, pale, very young rebel caught in a corner of organized collective society, where she is placed in the position of having to make her individual protest in defiance not of tyranny and oppression, but of good sense, logic and reasonableness of things-as-they-are.*

Worsley's analysis is lucid and exact. But he could not have made it on the basis of the American version, where the Chorus is allowed to state (with no warrant whatsoever from Anouilh) that Antigone incarnates "a passionate belief that moral law exists, and a passionate regard for the sanctity of human personality." Worsley, undistracted by any such claptrap, sees the real drama clearly:

> *This Creon is not a cruel tyrant; he has been called in to restore order in a country devastated by the gang warfare between his two nephews, Antigone's brothers. He is only anxious to save his niece ... He is eminently reasonable, but this kind of reason cannot convince her. And if she may not be able to change things-as-they-are, she can at least refuse to conform to them.*

> *She can, in the last analysis, refuse to be saved by them and this - against all sense, out of little more, when it is fined down, than an instinctive protest against life as it is - is what she does.*
>
> *This, then, is the progress of the play, the gradual whittling down, incident by incident, of her moral pretensions.*

IV. Since Galantière eventually showed himself capable of making an accurate translation, why did he not do so at first? And how did it then come about that, having made a free adaptation, he turned away from it three years later to observe stricter fidelity?

About his intentions regarding the 1946 version there is no doubt, since he explained them at some length in program notes for the New York production.[5] There he confessed to having introduced changes into the play, but claimed that they merely made some elements more emphatically clear. Creon's speeches, he said, were unaffected: "The lines are still M. Anouilh's." But while it was "important that we should hear (Creon's) arguments ... it was equally important to indicate that those arguments have no validity against a higher law .... This has been done, not by taking anything away from M. Anouilh's Creon, but by adding something to his Antigone, his Chorus, and his Haemon." In short, Galantière thought certain issues arising (in his interpretation) from the play needed magnifying and elaborating so that American audiences "would be able to come away from M. Anouilh's play with the feeling that Antigone's case was stronger than Creon's."

We can only speculate about reactions that may have induced him to discard that mistaken view. It is not improbable that Galantière was persuaded of the error of his ways by some vigilant reader of the original play who could see that close adherence to the French was necessary - not because of any scholastic purism, but simply because without that adherence the whole import of *Antigone* was being subverted.

CHAPTER 8

Problems of Propriety and Authenticity in Translating Modern Drama

ORTRUN ZUBER

Much has been written about the history and theory of translation, about applied translation, the stylistics of translation, and translation as linguistic comparison between systems.[1] I have deliberately restricted this paper to the problems of propriety and authenticity in translating modern drama.

To start with, translating a drama means facing most of the difficulties encountered in translating any other literary genre, considering semantic as well as cultural, historical and socio-political aspects, and also the form-content dichotomy. Not only the meaning of a word or sentence must be translated, but also the connotations, rhythm, tone and rhetorical level, imagery and symbols of association.

Rendering a dramatic work from one language and cultural background into another, moreover, means transposing the already translated text on to the stage. A play is written for a performance and must be actable. The audience must be able to understand it immediately and directly, and to accept it as an organic piece of work. The translation of a play requires more consideration of non-verbal and non-literary aspects than does the translation of novels or poetry. A play depends on additional elements, such as movements, gestures, postures, mimicry, speech rhythms, intonations, music and other sound effects, lights, stage scenery. In particular, a play is dependent on the immediacy of the impact on the audience.

Antonin Artaud and his followers proclaimed the theatre of gesture and a theatrical language which addresses our senses rather than the mind.

The greatest dramatists - such as Aeschylus, Sophocles, Euripides, Molière, Shakespeare - did not intend to write literature; they were writing for actors. Likewise, the translator of a play should not merely translate words and their meanings but produce speakable and performable translations. In the process of translating a play, it is necessary for him to mentally direct, act and see the play at the same time.

In the American theatre tradition, a play is not usually published in book form until it has proved successful on the stage. In rehearsals the text is constantly being changed by producers and actors in collaboration with the author. The degree of success of a play is determined first by "trying it out" in country towns and finally by the measurable financial returns of the "box-office". Thus, an American drama is a play, the frequently changed script for an effective stage performance, rather than an autonomous piece of literature.

Such a model would also seem to be appropriate in developing towards the published, final version of a play in translation: the translator's manuscript would first be tried out on the stage and discussed and changed in rehearsals, and only then published for future performances - or for readers. Ideally, the translator would be present at rehearsals and participate in the discussions and work of transferring the written translation on to the stage, because he alone has the most comprehensive awareness of the original and is uniquely qualified to advise on how to change and adapt the text or the stage directions, so that the dramatist's intention may always be maintained.

Two questions need clarifying at this point:

1. Why has the translated text to be tried out on the stage?

2. Why has the intention of the author of the original to be respected and maintained?

Let me attempt to answer the second question first: one may frequently hear the view that it is not crucial to maintain the dramatist's intention and the message of the original, but that a completely new work of art could emerge when trying to translate someone else's work, and that this translation might even surpass the original in artistic quality.

Indeed, in the past few years in Germany there has developed a strong tendency to modernize classical plays. Classical dramas have been completely rewritten, sometimes with little resemblance to the original, merely retaining the plot, or names etc.. There have been the controversial, revolutionary Shakespeare productions and free adaptations of other translated classics. Literary personages as well as those connected with the theatre have participated in this trend. These changes - whether radical or moderate, successful or unsuccessful, whether implemented by literati or by producers - are quite legitimate, provided that the author of the original is deceased. (He might well turn in his grave at certain productions, but he cannot interfere.)

It is a different matter if the dramatist is still alive, as the following case illustrates. There was an article in the *Frankfurter Allgemeine* (28 June, 1974) about a court case between Tennessee Williams and a theatre group in Berlin (Theater der Freien Volksbühne Berlin). The director, Charles Lang, had made some deliberate changes when producing *A Streetcar Named Desire*, e.g. the protagonist, the Polish-American Stanley Kowalski, was played by a black actor; the character of Eunice Hubbel and the first scene were eliminated completely, and the last two scenes were changed, in that Blanche was not raped by Stanley - as intended by Williams - but willingly agreed to the seduction. When Williams heard of this new production, he sent a telegram of protest through his agency (the International Famous Agency) to prevent the opening of the play. The State Court in Berlin then actually prohibited the opening for some time. On request, I was sent a copy of the procedures and decisions of the trial which, unlike most legal papers, provided fascinating reading. It was then that I became aware of the juridical limitations of translating a play and of transferring it into a different cultural setting.

Since this theatre company in Berlin was almost financially ruined at that time - which accounted for the omission of the first scene in which all minor characters appear - they had to agree to compromise and accept the decision of the Court. This meant that they could proceed, provided that certain changes would be made, namely, the negro's face had to be made up with white paint and his curly hair covered by a wig of straight hair. It is not difficult to imagine the disastrous outcome of this production and the half-hearted enthusiasm of the theatre group.

This example demonstrates simply, but dramatically, that there are limiting factors of propriety and authenticity which have to be considered when translating a modern drama.

Though the Federal State's Court conceded ".... that a producer is not merely the author's instrument, but may develop creative activity",[2] his creative talents have to submit to the dramatist's intention and to the message of his play. This is where Charles Lang went wrong. He made the mistake of confusing political and socio-psychological aspects, and of identifying the problem of racial discrimination with the problem of the American South. Tennessee Williams wanted to symbolize the latter by the characters of Blanche and Stanley; Blanche as a representative of aristocracy - once rich and cultured, now degenerate - and Stanley - the rough, vital upstart - as a symbol of rising democracy.

To sum up, the task of a translator as well as that of a producer of a modern play should be to transpose the play in such a manner, that the message of the original and the dramatist's intention be adhered to as closely as possible and be rendered, linguistically and artistically, into a form which takes into account the different traditional, cultural and socio-political background of the recipient country.

Let me return to the first question: why must the translated text be first tried out on the stage, before it can be accepted as the final version?

Even though a play might be perfectly translated linguistically, and even though it might be artistically refined, this piece of literature still requires action and movement in order to achieve that complete integration of text and performance, that coalescence of literature and theatre which constitutes drama. For example: a translator might have found the ideal verbal equivalent of a passage, but it turns out to be much longer in the target language. The stage directions require that this passage be spoken by a character in a raging, wild, violent, mood while moving from point A to point B on the stage. In our proposed translation he would reach point B, before having finished his speech. It would be rather awkward if he had to continue raging while standing still at point B. So the actor and producer - with the expert advice of the translator - have to decide whether it is more appropriate to slow down the motion, or to invent gestures carried out in rage at point B, or to move twice between A and B, or to shorten the text - whichever renders the dramatist's intention best. In this connection, it might be of interest to look at some findings of my dissertation in which I compared Tennessee Williams' *A Streetcar Named Desire* with the German translation by Berthold Viertel: *Endstation Sehnsucht*.

Reading the theatre reviews by American and German critics, it became quite obvious that *Streetcar* meant something different to the American audience than *Endstation* did to the German audience. In order to find the reasons for this discrepancy, I undertook, among other methods, a text comparison and analysis and encountered great problems with the text editions.

My first task, therefore, was to establish the authentic German text. The only German edition available then and now, was first published by Fischer Publishing Company in Frankfurt in 1954 together with the play *Glasmenagerie*. However, Berthold Viertel had translated *Streetcar* in 1949 for the German premières in Zürich in 1949 and in Berlin in 1950. So I had to establish which text had been used as the basis for these productions and all following productions up to 1954, when *Endstation* appeared as a Fischer paper back. In fact, it was a translation by Berthold Viertel mimeographed by the Theatre Department of the American High Commission in Bad Nauheim in 1949, but all copies had been confiscated and were, and still are, unavailable in bookshops and libraries. I could not consult Berthold Viertel on this matter, since he had died in 1953; therefore, I studied his literary estate in the archives of the Deutsches Literaturarchiv in Marbach.

There was no copy of the Bad Nauheim manuscript either. However, when I visited Berthold Viertel's widow in Vienna, she accidentally found the above-mentioned manuscript, yellowed, in one of her drawers. I borrowed the precious document for a day or so and found it to be exactly identical with the Fischer edition. And there is no other translation of *Streetcar* into German.

Having established which the authentic German text was, the next problem was to find the source for Berthold Viertel's translation. Neither the Fischer Publishing Company nor Tennessee Williams' agency nor Berthold Viertel's widow nor any of the many other people I contacted could advise me as to the American text which had been used.

According to Williams' bibliographer, Andreas Brown, the numerous editions of *Streetcar* in English can be traced back basically to three American editions:

1. *A Streetcar Named Desire,* New Directions, Norfolk, Connecticut, 1947, 1st - 4th printing.

2. *A Streetcar Named Desire,* New Directions, Revised Edition, 5th Printing, April 1950 (as well as all following printings).

3. *A Streetcar Named Desire,* Dramatists Play Service, Acting Edicion, 1953, revised version.

Andreas Brown, whom I visited in New York, explained that the first edition is the "pre-production" version, based on Williams' manuscript which he submitted before the première. Although the play was constantly changed in the course of the rehearsals by the producer, Elia Kazan, the actors and Williams himself, the manuscript was first published in the "pre-production" version by New Directions in four printings. Then the revised version or "production version" which complies with the première version and contains all changes was printed by New Directions from the fifth printing on. The third and final edition is the "post-production" version which Williams revised and amended for theatre groups and amateurs, especially in the detailed, technical stage directions.

The English editions all comply with the first American version except for the Signet edition which corresponds to the second American version. In Andreas Brown's view the third American edition, called the Acting Edition, can be considered definitive.

The question remains: which of these editions did Berthold Viertel use for his translation into German? It was essential to find the answer to this question, because you cannot begin a textual comparison and possibly accuse the translator of mistakes or misinterpretations, unless you know definitely *which* text he endeavoured to translate. As I mentioned before, not even Elisabeth Viertel-Neumann, who had typed the translation for her husband, could recall the exact title of the American text.

Therefore, I compared the text of the German translation with the three basic American editions and recognized an almost perfect congruence with the Acting Edition. However, because of the time discrepancy, Berthold Viertel in 1949 could not have had the Acting Edition itself, which did not appear until 1953, but possibly a precursor of the Acting Edition. Andreas Brown suspected that it must have been that manuscript, of which he once received a copy from Williams entitled: *A Streetcar Named Desire,* Broadway Production Script, Final Version, December 3, 1947 - Corrected January 3, 1949.

Indeed, I was able to verify Brown's assumption when, after a long search in the archives in Marbach, I found a small piece of yellowed newspaper with an article by Berthold Viertel in *Die Neue Zeitung,* München, 10.5.1950, stating that the translator followed the "final version" of the Broadway Production Script. I traced a copy of this script in the Humanities Research Centre at the University of Texas, and, by textual comparison, ascertained the identicality of this script with the Acting Edition - with only minor deviations in the stage directions and in a few words or idiomatic expressions, e.g.

Final Version	Acting Edition
representing the L & N railroad tracks (p. 1-1-1)	*suggesting railroad tracks (p. 5)*
couch (P. 1-1-2)	*day-bed (p. 6)*
bureau (p. 1-1-10)	*dressing table (p. 12)*
photograph (p. 1-1-13)	*photo (p. 14)*
picture (p. 1-1-14)	*photo (p. 14)*
Blanche is bathing (p. 1-2-21)	*Blanche is in bathroom, taking a bath (p. 19).*

Final Version	Acting Edition
Blanche comes around the corner at R, and approaches the women on the spiral stair, carrying her suitcase in her left hand. The lights in the street commence to dim, and the interior lighting in the apartment brightens. (p. 1-1-13)	*Blanche comes around corner at R, and approaches the women on spiral stair, carrying suitcase in her l. hand. Lights in street commence to dim, and interior lighting in apartment brightens. (p. 7)*

Thus, the verbatim text comparison finally established the identity of this manuscript with the Acting Edition - apart from the few insignificant changes of words or condensations in the stage directions mentioned. It was then established that the first German translation (the Bad Nauheim manuscript, 1949) is identical with the Fischer paperback edition (1954), and that the American production script (Final Version, 1947, revised 1949), which served as the translation submission, is largely identical with the Acting Edition (1953) in all major respects.

It is regrettable, however, that Berthold Viertel did not have at his disposal the reading editions by New Directions as well, because they contain detailed descriptions of the characters, attuning the reader, (i.e. also the German producer and actors and subsequently the audience) to the atmosphere and thereby supplying interpretation aids for the problems, atmosphere and the characters of the play. These interpretation aids are therefore missing in the German version.

Also missing is the motto, which could transmit the author's unambiguous view and could help prevent misinterpretations frequently to be found in German reviews:

And so it was I entered the broken world
To trace the visionary company of love, its voice
An instant in the wind (I know not whither hurled)
But not for long to hold each desperate choice.

'The Broken Tower' by Hart Crane

Und so betrat ich die zerbrochene Welt,
die erträumte Gemeinschaft der Liebe aufzuspüren,
ihre Stimme klang einen Augenblick im Wind
(ich weiss nicht wohin geweht),
doch niemals das verzweiflungsvoll Gewählte
für lange festzuhalten.

Further reasons why *Endstation* in Germany was interpreted differently to *Streetcar* in America are to be found in the linguistic translation. When Berthold Viertel translated *Streetcar* in 1949, he was probably not aware of the effects which his translation would have on readers and audiences in Germany for decades. He was only trying to meet the people's demands at that time after the war and after being cut off from other cultures, ideas and literatures for so long - he was only trying to meet the demand to translate as many plays as possible in as short a time as possible. His widow told me that he translated *Streetcar* in 3-4 weeks dictating to her the text freely from the American manuscript as she typed. He hardly ever used a dictionary, only occasionally looking up uncommon or slang expressions. First and foremost, she said, he translated *Streetcar* - just as he did the other plays - for performance purposes and - as I understood from reading his correspondence held in the Deutsches Literaturarchiv - for financial reasons. It is interesting, though, to note that Berthold Viertel made many changes and deletions in his production script which, incidentally, was a copy of the Bad Nauheim manuscript. He made these changes - almost all of them improvements - when he directed *Streetcar* himself for the first time in Berlin in 1950. Unfortunately, these improvements only had an effect on the performances produced by Berthold Viertel himself, because they were never published and therefore not available to other directors or producers. When I asked Elisabeth Viertel-Neumann why her late husband in 1953 had submitted the manuscript of his first translation of 1949 and not that of his second revised version of 1950 to Fischer for publication, she explained that he had been working on several projects at that time (i.e. in 1953, including the translation of *Camino Real*, and the revision and production of *Antony and Cleopatra*) and that he had already been ill. Hence, he was no longer occupied with *Streetcar* and simply sent off the completed Bad Nauheim manuscript to Fischer rather than having the revised version re-typed and proof-read. It thus happened that all subsequent performances of *Endstation* in Germany have been based on the first, unrevised translation of 1949 by Berthold Viertel.

Considering the conditions mentioned above, Berthold Viertel's translation achievement is truly outstanding. Yet we cannot overlook the fact that his haste allowed many mistakes to slip in - mistakes which caused misunderstandings and misinterpretations, many of which he later corrected while involved with this play more intensively on a second occasion, namely as the producer of the Berlin production.

I scrutinized Berthold Viertel's corrections in his production script for the Berlin premiere which is held in the Theatre Museum in Vienna. His changes in many cases convert the meaning of a sentence into the complete opposite; other corrections refer to mistakes of grammar, idiomatic expressions, usage, style, level of speech, semantics etc.. Let me give you just one example, namely the translation of two lines from a sonnet by Elizabeth Browning engraved on Mitch's cigarette case, once given to him by a late girl friend whom he had loved:

I shall but love thee better after death (p. 58)	*Werd ich Dich nach dem Tod Nur um so besser lieben* (p. 36)

In his Berlin production script Berthold Viertel corrected "besser" to "mehr". "Besser lieben" in German definitely means "to make love in a better way" and refers to improving sexual techniques, whereas "mehr lieben" conveys deeper genuine love, which is intended here. Williams used these lines, read out by Blanche, as an artistic device to symbolically emphasize Blanche's desire, hopes and attitude towards life. She is looking for a relationship different from that between Stan and Stella, which is based on physical attraction. Blanche tries to find a relationship which does not demand depersonalization, but which is based on psychic, spiritual, mutual love and understanding.

Williams made extensive use of many other devices, symbols and signs of association to make Blanche's view of life quite clear, but in many instances their meanings are lost in the German translation or even reversed. Consequently, German critics have often described Blanche as being arrogant and malicious, a psychiatric case, a hypocrite and a liar; they did not share their American counterparts' pity and understanding for her tragic fall.

I think a complete revision of the German translation would be desirable and worthwhile, since this play has become a modern classic and been very successful and popular in Germany, despite the present unrevised edition. Frau Viertel, who is still receiving the royalties for *Endstation* said that she, too, would be in favour of a revised edition.

For such a revised German edition I would make the following suggestions:

1. As a basis for revision, one could use Berthold Viertel's translation (Bad Nauheim 1949, Fischer Publishers 1954) together with his corrections in his production script for the Berlin première - held in the Theatre Museum in Vienna.

2. As the translation source, one should use the American production script (Final Version 1947, revised 1949; Acting Edition 1953) as well as the reading edition (New Directions from 5th printing) especially for the character descriptions and stage directions, which would mean an extension of Berthold Viertel's translation.

3. As an appendix or in a separate handbook one could offer the following aids:

   (a) A sketch of the set stage picture by Ita Maximowna (Berlin production script);

   (b) a sketch of lighting directions worked out by Berthold Viertel in his Berlin production script;

   (c) a list of costumes for the main characters in all scenes;

   (d) sources of supply for records and tapes with the background noises (e.g. cat screams, train, chimes, police siren, crowd, thunder on records, available from the Dramatists Play Service) and with the music. Herbert Baumann, who was the music director for the Berlin production, could be consulted for the production of a music tape, likewise Berthold Viertel's notes in his Berlin script in which he lists all pieces of music.

4. Other additional changes might be made by the reviser of the new German edition, at his/her discretion.

I hope I have shown that the transposition of a modern drama from one language and cultural background into another raises problems of propriety and authenticity, which must be faced. And I hope to have shown that the solution of these problems may lie partly in trying out the translated version on the stage before publishing a definitive edition and in respecting and maintaining the intention of the author of the original.

CHAPTER 9

Henrik Ibsen in English Translation

MAY BRIT AKERHOLT

As both poet and dramatist Henrik Ibsen paid great attention to his language. One of his main characteristics is the short but full phrase, the ability to produce sentences pregnant with meaning without a superfluous word. Another typical feature is the constant variation in tone and style to which a translator must be alert, as they characterise, and emphasise changes in action. In dealing with the English versions of Ibsen's plays, there are two main aspects which need to be considered closely.

Firstly there are mistranslations and misinterpretations which invariably occur in translations and which reflect on the treatment of themes and imagery. These aspects are illustrated by comparing two English translations of *Peer Gynt* to the original. This play is exceedingly rich in symbolism and imagery as well as in language. The added problems of a rhymed verse drama, such as alliteration, assonance, phonetic effects, rhythm and rhyme also make it an interesting work to discuss from the point of view of translation.

Secondly there are the differences which exist between languages. Each language has its own modes of expression and its lingual peculiarities. These reflect, of course, on style as well. Problems of language and style are discussed in relation to translations of some of Ibsen's later prose dramas, where the language is precise and exact, and where certain aspects of it are used for specific purposes.

I

A study of *Peer Gynt* necessarily involves comments on language and style as they are important parts of a verse drama and in so far as they are relevant to the interpretation of the play. However, the main emphasis is on the effects of mistranslation on themes, imagery and matters of interpretation. Because of its rich symbolism, abundance of characters and themes and full measure of local colour, *Peer Gynt* is particularly suitable to use as a demonstration in regards to this aspect of translation.

The two English versions which will be dealt with here represent contrasting methods of approach to the problems of translating Ibsen. R. Farquharson Sharp's translation of 1921[1] keeps close to the original with an old-fashioned style and a "faithful-to-Ibsen" direct translation at times. He has closely followed the various changes in rhythm. The language has a tendency to be awkward and heavy, he uses too many words and often lacks the supple and infinitely elegant and concise phrase that Ibsen mastered to perfection, even in a verse drama so rich in language as *Peer Gynt*. Michael Meyer's translation of 1963[2] is in free verse and modern in style. There are times when Ibsen's play is unrecognisable, not so much in the single line, phrase or scene, but in the overall tone provided by the modern language. But there are many fine passages as well, with easy-flowing rhythms and precise language in Ibsenian style.

The opening scene demonstrates Ibsen's extraordinary command of the language and his poetical powers. The first half of the first scene is taken up with Ase and Peer. The poetry is terse and the pace is fast; the tone is both colloquial and poetic and verse, language and meaning are closely connected. Alliteration and assonance emphasise the content and, together with the even rhythm and regular but varied rhymes, urge the reader forward with the speed of the buck and Peer as they fly through the air. The opening passage is strong and takes us right into Peer's fantasy world. The first three lines are a perfect example of the way dialogue is used throughout. Ase opens and stops in midline, Peer completes the line, a new full line from Ase, then Peer stops in the middle of his next line, which Ase finishes with a rhyme on Peer's first line. This form of dialogue links and separates the characters as well as the actions and is used in various ways. A single line may be divided between as many as three characters with three internal rhymes, as in the Haegstad scene, where it gives emphasis to the content and illustrates the atmosphere and the unanimous mood of the people. In the opening passage the break is in midline and the lines flow on, conveying a sense of symmetry and of equal importance to both characters. It is like an even duel between mother and son. A few lines further down the division is more marked. Ase has most of the line; she is still ironic and doubtful and is breaking into Peer's tale. But he takes over with two short, forceful words: "Det smalt" (It cracked) and from then on the story is his.

A free verse translation must necessarily differ a great deal from a verse drama which uses rhythm as well as rhyme to emphasise, diversify and unite. Meyer's corresponding passage alternates between short and long lines, but there is little left of the original dialogue pattern and there are no phonetic sound changes, alliteration or assonance. Farquharson Sharp has conveyed Ibsen's dialogue form quite well, but all divisions occur in mid-line. There is no evident change in the phonetic pattern, nor any emphasis on alliteration or assonance. The absence of these details together with the lack of rhymes in the two English translations tend to lessen the strong impact of the opening passage.

The women in Peer's life shape his fate to a great extent. Ingrid at Haegstad, the Troll Princess and Anitra are outlets for his selfish and lower instincts; Solveig is the shining symbol of woman and motherhood, the goal at the end of the journey. But it is Ase who made him what he is, who brought a world of fairytales and imagination into their poor farmhouse, who showed him a means of escape from the cold, hard facts. She is despairing at his tall stories and lack of responsibility, but she never gives up all hope for him:

> *Gid du bare ble sa klok,*
> *at du engang kunne bøte*
> *flengen i din egen brok!*
>
> (If you only became so wise,
> that you once could mend
> the tear in your own breeches!)[3]

These are ambiguous words. She is referring in exasperation to his torn clothes, but mixed with some of the snorting of her previous line "You!" there is an overtone of wishful hoping, implying something like "if you only could grow up enough to be able to see and repair that wildness of yours, to turn that imagination to better use and give your strength to more worth-while matters". The English translations are not satisfactory and show the tendency of the one translator to use too many and the other too few words. Meyer's compressed line is only scornful, a repetition of the "You!": "You'll learn to mend your breeches first!" (p.35) Farquharson Sharp has caught some of the flavour, but his last line ignores the spirit of the passage and seems to be quite superfluous:

If you ever know enough
To mend your breeches when they're torn
'Tis the most that I could hope for. (p. 11)

Peer returns from his exile in the forest to find his mother dying. Ase lies in the same small bed that Peer used as a child. In those days they were pretending that the bed was a sleigh with the mother as the driver and the son as the passenger, riding away into the land of fairytales. The roles are reversed as Peer rides Ase into heaven on his imaginary Grane. In Meyer the rug becomes the sleigh, and while this is not a serious mistake he should have observed the symbolism of the bed as the escape-valve used by mother and son both then and now. Peer tries to give back to Ase what she has always given him: an escape from the ugly reality. It is perhaps a cowardly way out but it is the only one he knows. The imaginary crowd cheers them in the castle in heaven, just as the people greeted Emperor Peer on his horse in the sky. But Ase is frightened and uneasy:

ASE: *Kjaere Peer, du kjφrer vel rett?*

PEER: *Her er brede veien.*

(Dear Peer, you drive right, don't you?
Here the road is broad.)

The dialogue is ambiguous: "rett" means both "the right way" and "straight", and the special construction of Peer's line indicates both interpretations as well. The passage must be considered together with the judgement that is passed on Peer in the last act by Ase's voice in the air, where the ambiguity is made clear as both meanings are included:

ASE'S
VOICE: *Tvi, for en skyssgutt!*
Hu, du har veltet meg!
......
Galt har du kjφrt meg,
Peer, hvor er slottet?

(Fie, what a driver!
Ugh, you have overturned me!)
......
(Wrong have you driven me,
Peer, where is the castle?)

Neither translator has achieved this ambiguity in the first passage; they have actually conveyed one meaning each. Meyer implies that he did not drive straight and so overturned:

ASE: *Peer, dear, are you driving carefully?*

PEER: *The road's broad here.* *(p. 86)*

and Farquharson Sharp that he took the wrong way:

ASE: *Are you sure you know the way?*

PEER: *I can see the road.* *(p. 101)*

Meyer's second passage contains both meanings:

You're a fine driver!
Look where you've thrown me
......
You've come the wrong way!
Oh, Peer, where's the castle? *(p. 158)*

while Farquharson Sharp's last line is obscure:

Fie, what a driver!
Ugh! You've upset me
......
Peer, where's the Castle?
You've driven madly; (p. 206)

What does he mean by "madly"? Carelessly or wrongly? He achieves the ambiguity here where the two meanings should be made clear.

The two translators show a disregard for the importance of repetition as a means of emphasis and parallel. Two examples have to suffice in showing the relevance of the way Ibsen uses repetition. In the beginning when Ase realises that Peer has tricked her with the story of the buckride she curses him:

O din fandens reglesmed;
......
Remsen, som du kommer med,

(Oh, you devil of a tale-teller;
......
The tale you're coming up with,)

In Meyer's version she is swearing:

Oh, you bloody story-teller! ......
I remember now, I heard all this rubbish
Before, (p. 32)

There is a difference between the two. "Devil" has connotations of darkness and evil, of something that takes over the good part of us. But mainly the lines are important because of the words "remse, regle", identical in meaning and repeated on several occasions. It is difficult to find an English word which covers them completely. "Tale" is perhaps the closest one can come; it conveys imagination, story-telling and something invented by the narrator. Meyer translates "remse" with "all this rubbish" which is an unfortunate choice. Peer's story is taken from folklore that Ase knows and respects. Farquharson Sharp's "rigmarole" is better but has too much of a sense of "nonsense" in it. When the word is used ironically by the crowd at Haegstad commenting on Peer's tale, Meyer fails to keep the link while Farquharson

Sharp does by repeating "rigmarole". Meyer's "rubbish" in the first case becomes "yarn" in the second. But it is, at least, a change for the better. The same word plays a significant role in Ase's death scene. There it is *she* who talks about Peer's buckride as a reality and *he* who calls it a tale:

PEER: *Ja, ja; la den reglen fare.*
(Yes, yes; leave that tale alone)

It is a pity that the translators fail to continue the link:

Yes, well, never mind that. (Meyer, p. 83)

Never mind all that nonsense and rubbish;
(Farquharson Sharp, p. 96)

It is both ironic and sad to remember Peer's earlier confession about the ride: "Fake and damned lie!". But Peer's admission is to the fact that it did not happen to him, not that the tale itself is a piece of rubbish.

In the beginning of Act V Peer is a vicious old man with no consideration for others and with the same ambition to succeed, to outshine, still alive inside him. Struggling to keep afloat on the hull of a dinghy after the ship sinks Peer saves his own life by sacrificing the cook. The key-word in the two men's dialogue is "vik" (yield, give way):

PEER: ....*Hvelvet baer ei to!*

COOK: *Det vet jeg. Vik!*

PEER: *Vik selv!*

(......The hull doesn't carry two!
I know that. Yield!
Yield yourself!)

In the Norwegian version of the Bible Christ said to the Tempter in the

Wilderness: "Vik fra meg, Satan" (Yield from me, Satan). Five times in the play Peer uses this phrase. It is connected either with Peer finding himself at the end of the rope or with his being afraid of his past sins coming to the surface. It first occurs when the woman, the former greenclad princess, and her troll child appear outside Solveig's cottage:

Vik fra meg, din trollheks!
(Yield from me, you trollwitch!)

He says it twice to the Strange Passenger who wants his body for dissection to examine the seat of his dreams:

Vik fra meg!
Vik fra meg, skremsel!
(scarecrow, monster)

and finally to the Button Moulder who wants to erase him completely:

Vik, Satan!

A case like this obviously presents difficulties to an English translator who cannot very well use "Satan" every time to keep the biblical implication, nor can he employ "get thee behind me" which would seem conspicuously out of place in some of the phrases. Meyer and Farquharson Sharp have relinquished the repetition of "vik" and its implications, probably to make room for a more varied language, perhaps to the benefit of each phrase in itself but to the detriment of the play seen as a whole. Their phrases vary from place to place: "Get away, you old witch!"; "Get out"; "Get off yourself!"; "Leave me, you bug bear!"; "Get away!" (Farquharson Sharp). "Get away, you witch!"; "Away!"; "You get off!"; "Get away! You frighten me!"; "Get behind me, Satan!" (Meyer). But it is important to keep the connection between the passages and I suggest that a translator should make use of the same verbal expression throughout.

The satire in *Peer Gynt* is aimed at what Dovregubben, the King of Trolls, calls "the trollish-nationalistic". Ibsen wanted to shake the Norwegians out of what he saw as an escape from reality into a fairytale-world of dreams and wishful hoping for a revival of the great past. The result, as interpreted by him, was national and individual narrow-minded complacency. Like the trolls of the steep mountains they went around with their heads in the clouds.

The meeting between Man and Troll in the Dovrehall could have been a turning point for Peer, but he is too engrossed in himself to see the real truth in the difference between Man's philosophy and the Trolls' philosophy as expressed by Dovregubben:

> *Mann, vaer deg selv!*
> *Troll, vaer deg selv - nok!*
>
> (Man, be yourself!
> Troll, be yourself - enough!)

They are in direct opposition: man, be true to yourself; troll, be true only to your own selfish needs. In his notes Meyer explains the latter phrase as "to be self-sufficient in a bad sense". This is not accurate enough as the sense of complacency, self-satisfaction is just as important as that of self-sufficiency. The continuous theme of the megalomania displayed in Peer's royal dreams intermingles with the theme "be thyself/ be thyself enough".

Farquharson Sharp's translation of the philosophies is the classical one, used by most translators; it adequately conveys the right meaning:

> *Man, to thyself be true!*
> *Troll, to thyself be - enough.* *(p. 62)*

I have reservations about Meyer's version:

> *Man, be thyself!*
> *Be thyself - Jack!* *(p. 63)*

An incongruity is created in the troll motto by the use of the old-fashioned "thyself" with a flippant slang expression. Moreover, it leaves out the word "enough" and the crucial idea of the egotism expressed by it. This word is being played on throughout the drama, and because of his paraphrase

Meyer has himself pointed out that he has had to rewrite Ibsen's phrases in some of the places where "enough" occurs, notably in Act V where it is used several times by itself.

Peer's misconception of the philosophies is apparent in all his actions and behaviour. He constantly mixes up the two mottos:

Hva skal mannen vaere!
Seg selv; *det er mitt korte svar.*
Om seg *og* sitt *han skal seg kjaere.*

(What should man be!
Himself; that is my short answer.
Take care of *himself* and what is *his*.)

His arrogant explanation of the Gyntian Self is in ironic conflict with the true meaning of Self and the reality which is gradually revealed to him:

Det gyntske selv, - *det er den haer*
av ϕnsker, lyster og begjaer, -

(The Gyntian *Self* - it is the host
of desires, wishes, lust,)

Returning home as an old man Peer discovers that his name does live, not as the splendid King of his life's dreams, but yet as a kind of legend, the Peer of the folktale Ibsen got the name from, the roguish story-teller, the unbridled youth:

Den grakledde: A sludder; blodet er aldri sa tynt,
en kjenner seg alltid i slekt med Peer Gynt.

(Man in grey: Oh, nonsense; the blood is never so thin,
one always feels a relationship to Peer Gynt.)

Unfortunately, Farquharson Sharp has mistranslated the passage:

Oh, nonsense! Blood is thicker than that;
At least we're both Peer Gynt's relations. (p. 196)

It seems he is referring to the talk about brothers-in-law and relations earlier in the scene. The meaning is universal, though; the blood is never so thin that one doesn't feel akin to Peer Gynt. It is a kick to the Norwegians and their Gyntian characteristics; there is a little of Peer in everyone, especially in the nationalistic selfishness of "being oneself enough".

The Button Moulder's mission in life is to recast useless people like Peer Gynt. *His* definition of what it is to be yourself is a strikingly ironic contrast to Peer's own:

> *A vaere seg selv, er: seg selv a dϕde*
> ......
> *overalt a mϕde*
> *med Mesters mening til uthengsskilt.*
>
> (To be oneself, is: oneself to kill
> ......
> everywhere to live
> in accordance with the Master's intention.)[4]

The definition is enigmatic and must be seen in context with several other passages, particularly the priest's burial speech, the Thin Person's strange talk about positive and negative pictures and the dialogues between Peer and the Button Moulder throughout the last act. The full meaning of what it is to be oneself can only be found in the play as a whole. Basically Ibsen's meaning is this: we must mortify the inferior self, suppress our baser instincts and let the true self, the noble self come to the surface. Peer believes he has always been himself and does not understand that he suppressed his potentially good qualities, letting his baser self take over. The translators have chosen different ways of expressing the Button Moulder's explanation:

> *To be one's self is to slay one's self*
> ......
> *To follow out in everything,*
> *What the Master's intention was.* (Farquharson Sharp, p. 223)

To be oneself is: to kill oneself
...... always to serve the Master's intention.
(Meyer, p. 168)

Either "one's self" or "oneself" can be taken to mean the inferior or the superior self. Only the context defines the meaning of the term "seg selv". To bring out the concept of the Button Moulder's definition as clearly as possible, however, the apostrophe may be used in one place and left out in the other. That way one makes a distinction between the two selves. Farquharson Sharp's choice of "slay" is wrong because of its strong implication of the physical act. Ibsen's old-fashioned "døde" has more of the figurative sense of mortify than of slay.

Peer is frantically running around trying to save himself from being melted down to nothingness, revisiting old places and memories. Wherever he goes he finds proof that he has been "a nothing" in the Button Moulder's sense. He suffers from the fact that he lived after the trolls' philosophy no matter how much he believed he was true to himself in the right way. Ironically, the Button Moulder states that Peer *did* have the right potentials once:

Du *var nu etlet til en blinkende knapp*
pa verdensvesten; men hempen glapp;

(*You* were intended to be a gleaming button
on the world's waistcoat; but the loop slipped).

Farquharson Sharp has mistranslated one word and thereby lost the whole idea:

Now you
Were meant to be a gleaming button
On the world's waistcoat, but your loop was missing. (p. 211)

The loop slipped, or broke; it was not missing from the beginning as implied here. This is vital to the whole point. In one way the lines are a reflection on the magnitude of Peer's "crime" against his self; he was, after all, born to shine in this world. In another way it indicates that the blame is not fully his. The loop slipped, he did not let it go on purpose. Circumstances, upbringing, Ase herself were all contributing forces, helping him to take the wrong direction at the cross-roads.

II

In considering style and language there are two main pitfalls to be avoided by translators. To be faithful to the original text to the extent of not missing a word or turn of phrase may easily result in an old-fashioned style, elaborate and rather awkward which makes it difficult to retain the universality of Ibsen's work. This is the case with the pioneer of Ibsen translations, William Archer.[5] In his strict obedience to the original he brought an artificiality to the English language as if he translated word for word from Norwegian. The text becomes rhetorical and lacks the easy-flowing colloquial tone and simple lucidity of Ibsen's prose. On the other hand, if the language is full of modern slang or is too modernised in its overall style, the translator faces the danger of turning the characters into people of our modern society. The public knows it is not dealing with a contemporary author, and a modern way of speech in an otherwise 19th century setting may create paradoxical situations which will only confuse.

Una Ellis-Fermor clearly states that she translates for a modern public, virtually pretending that Ibsen wrote his plays in the 1950's. She also makes a few changes to props and costumes, "in order not to confuse the reader or transport him suddenly to the Victorian world"[6], claiming the modern reader visualises the figures in modern dress. The reader, as well as the theatre audience, is already in the Victorian world, put there by detailed stage descriptions and by the setting. The product of such an attempt could easily belong to the category Miss Ellis-Fermor herself calls "that safe and colourless neutrality".[7] To a certain extent this has happened to her translations. One example will illustrate this point. In *The Wild Duck* there is a slightly pompous but very elegant line spoken by the fat guest at Werle's dinner party:

Men herre gud, er det sant at De har
opphevet den velsignede røkefrihet?

(But good God, is it true that you have
abolished the blessed smoking freedom?)

This line belongs in the drawing-rooms of the 19th century. Ellis-Fermor's version is rather awkward and a mixture of old and new:

Now, now! Is it true that you've done
away with that pleasant privilege
of smoking where we liked? (p. 150)

This line is well translated by Rolf Fjelde:[8]

But really, is it true you've abolished
our precious smoking privilege? (p. 126)

And by James McFarlane:[9]

But, I say, is it true you have abolished
our precious freedom to smoke? (p. 117)

Whether a translator chooses to modernise Ibsen or not he will have to tackle a few basic problems. The most obvious one is the Norwegian distinction between the plural and singular form of second person (du/thou-De/you). It cannot be ignored considering its relevance to matters of interpretation. Ibsen deliberately uses the two forms to distinguish between nuances in speech and to stress intimacy or distance in relationships. For example, when the Stranger meets Ellida in the last act of *A Lady from the Sea* he uses the intimate "du" which clearly emphasises the close relationship they once had. This is strengthened by the previous scene with Bolette and Arnholm who have decided to get married but still say the formal "De" to each other. Ellida, however, addresses the Stranger as "De", thereby implying that their involvement has changed, at least on her part. It also points forward to her choice to stay with her husband. When she does choose, the Stranger switches to "De". They are now truly estranged and he goes back to the sea. The Stranger's use of Ellida's first name throughout has also stressed their former closeness. Archer turns this to his advantage and partly solves the problem by letting the Stranger disappear with a "Good-bye, Mrs. Wangel".[10] In the translations of Peter Watts[11] and McFarlane, however, the Stranger's departing line is a short "good-bye" and the subtle but significant use of the personal pronoun is lost. It should be added that this is not compensated for by other means, as changes in tone or style, for example.

Forms of address play an important part in *Hedda Gabler*. Hedda and Mr. Brack call each other "De", but familiarity is hinted at in Mr. Brack's use of her Christian name, kept respectable by the addition of "fru" (Mrs, Madam). The strained relationship between Hedda and Jφrgen Tesman's aunt is seen in Hedda's formal "De" and "Miss Tesman" and in the latter's avoidance of the personal pronoun.[12] Her lines are so cleverly worked out that it seems quite natural for her to say "Hedda", "Hedda Gabler", "Hedda Tesman" or just "child" even in direct conversation. It gives her lines a peculiar flavour, adding to her characterisation and slightly emphasising the strain between them. There is, of course, not the same need to avoid "you" in English; for one thing this is difficult in a language which has expressions like "thank you". Consequently this small but still significant point is to some extent lost in English versions. It is, however, possible to construct Miss Tesman's speech so that "you" is consistently left out in her direct address to Hedda, thereby retaining the essence of the special quality of her lines and the suggestion of a strained relationship.

Hedda is strictly formal with Eilert Lφvborg but allows him to use her first name when they are alone. A tricky situation occurs when Hedda rebukes him for calling her "du":

> *Blir De ved a si du til meg,*
> *sa vil jeg ikke tale med Dem.*
>
> (If you continue to say "du" to me,
> I won't talk to you.)

Lφvborg asks if he can say "du" when no one else is present but Hedda refuses; he may think it but never say it. From then on Lϕvborg calls her "De" even if he continues to say "Hedda". This incident has been dealt with unsatisfactorily in many English translations. Ellis-Fermor lets Hedda forbid Lϕvborg to call her "my dear"; a solution of a kind but a dubious one since "dear" seems to be employed by most of the characters in different situations, whether they "De" or "du" each other. The versions of Fjelde and Eva Le Gallienne[13] seem adequate at first glance; both have Hedda deny Lϕvborg the use of her first name. Unfortunately, they have not followed through the consequences of their paraphrase. Lϕvborg keeps calling her "Hedda", which is quite improbable as she has expressly forbidden it in their versions.

The numerous Norwegian particles pose another problem as it is often difficult to find apt equivalents in English. These words are frequently linked with the tone of a line. Colloquial or formal tone may depend on the choice of small or seemingly insignificant words. Two examples will show how two translators have solved different meanings of the expression "dog vel" (perhaps, however) in Act I of *A Doll's House*. Krogstad has arrived to ask Nora to use her influence with Helmer on his behalf:

> ...... *De har dog vel tid*
> *et ϕyeblikk?*
>
> (...... you have perhaps time
> for a moment?)

Here the "dog vel" conveys a feeling of undertainty and appeal, more so than the English "perhaps" can do. Fjelde has managed to capture that sense:

> ...... *You do have a moment*
> *to spare, I suppose?* *(p. 62)*

McFarlane's translation does not have that tone of appeal:

...... You've got a moment
to spare? *(p. 131)*

Nora is relieved he did not come about the money she owes him and quite casually answers his questions about Mrs. Linde's appointment at the bank:

A, man har dog vel alltid en liten
smule innflytelse, skulle jeg tro ...

(Oh, one has perhaps a tiny
bit of influence, I should think ......)

"Dog vel alltid" (alltid/always) mainly stresses the casualness of her reply; again not quite the meaning of "perhaps". It also gives her line a slight overtone of aloofness, even of superiority. Fjelde's version conveys the right mixture:

NORA: *Oh, one does have a tiny bit of*
influence, I should hope. *(p. 63)*

So does McFarlane's line, but it lacks the elegance of Ibsen's style:

NORA: *Oh, I think I can say that some of us have a*
little influence now and again. *(p. 132)*

The quality of Ibsen translations need to be improved. They generally fail to convey a sense of the finer nuances, as the translators seem to lack the intimate knowledge of the language which is necessary to bring out the ambiguity of a sentence, the subtle use of imagery or the different meanings a word or an expression can have in certain circumstances. Direct mistranslations causing misrepresentations are unnecessary and should be possible to eliminate. In many cases too little attention is paid to the interrelation between language, theme and imagery, resulting in diminished impact as well as loss of important points of interpretation. Ibsen's way of using language, blending style, dialogue and action with devices like repetition, ambiguity and irony to make a united whole is weakened in English translations.

CHAPTER 10

Problems in Translating Sean O'Casey's Drama *Juno and the Paycock* into German

UTE VENNEBERG

Between April 1923 and February 1926 five plays by Sean O'Casey opened at the Abbey in Dublin, among them *Juno and the Paycock* on March 3, 1924.[1] It was the first play in the twenty-year history of the Abbey to be extended for a second week.[2] While it is true that the first performance of *The Shadow of a Gunman* a year before had already proved to be a great success, it was *Juno and the Paycock* which confirmed O'Casey's fame as a playwright. The play, first published together with *The Shadow of a Gunman* in 1925,[3] and for which O'Casey received the Hawthornden Prize in London in 1926, is regularly produced in the repertoire of various kinds of theatres today.[4]

Although a lot of studies dealing with general and specific aspects of O'Casey's dramatic works have been published,[5] the problems involved in translating them into German and performing them in German theatres have not yet been sufficiently analysed.[6] These problems should be thoroughly investigated, because the translations have had a crucial influence on the reception of O'Casey's plays in German-speaking countries.[7]

The German premiere of *Juno and the Paycock* did not take place until 1953, when Ernst Ginsberg directed the play in Munich under the title *Juno und der Pfau*.[8] A translation by Georg Goyert, which had been revised by Erwin Kalser and Ernst Ginsberg, served as the basis for the performance. For the presentation of *Juno and the Paycock* at the municipal theatre in Wuppertal, Gert Otmar Leutner revised the original translation by Georg Goyert. Since then, the version of Erwin Kalser and Ernst Ginsberg has not been performed, which is not to say that Leutner's version was henceforth regarded as an "official" translation of *Juno and the Paycock*. It was only used when Leutner himself directed the play.

The fact that the German performing rights were controlled by several publishers, who now and then authorized translators and directors to translate the plays or adapt existing German versions, may be regarded as one of the reasons why there was a general shortage of translations in the beginning and why the existing ones were only of very poor quality. And the fact that German audiences took such little interest in O'Casey's plays can probably be ascribed to the want and to the inadequate form of the translations.

Since the East-German "Henschelverlag" publishing house in Berlin and the "Suhrkamp Theater-Verlag" in Frankfurt/Main obtained the only German performing rights in 1968, more translations have become available, not only for producers, but also for German-speaking readers.[9] In 1966 the "Aufbau-Verlag" in East Berlin and Weimar had already published a translation of *Juno and the Paycock* in a selected anthology of O'Casey's plays.[10] This translation was reprinted without any changes in the same year by the "Diogenes Verlag" in Zurich, which controls the publishing rights for West Germany, Austria and Switzerland, and again by the "Aufbau-Verlag" in 1976.[11] In 1973 the "Henschelverlag" brought out a translation by Maik Hamburger and Adolf Dresen. It was first presented in Graz, Austria, in 1969. Today, German performances of *Juno and the Paycock* have to use this translation, as it is now the only authorized version. The Hamburger-Dresen translation was also reprinted by the "Diogenes Verlag"[12], and is the result of a "translation project" between the "Henschelverlag" and the "Suhrkamp Theater-Verlag".

The details given above are necessary in that they provide an impression of the history of the German translations of *Juno and the Paycock*. They also show that non-verbal aspects, such as the question of performing rights and publishing rights, have to be considered when dealing with translation problems and comparing different versions, especially when studying the problems of translating plays by Sean O'Casey into German.

There are some generally accepted rules and principles, which are often referred to in studies on problems of translating plays. The first principle is that translations for the stage should be "speakable", or in the words of Max Beerbohm: "... there is a great difference between what looks well in type and what sounds well on a pair of lips ..."[13] This principle demands that the sentences and semantic units, later spoken and interpreted by the actors, should not be too long to be understood by an audience. An audience occupies a different position than, for example, the reader of a book, who can decide where to stop and reflect upon the words he is confronted with. A second rule says that the translation as a whole should not become longer than the original version. This is a constant problem when translating from English into German. In addition to the dialogue and stage direction, non-verbal elements, such as scenery, the shape of the stage, properties, costumes, lights and colours, which often function as symbols and address the audience intellectually or emotionally, must also be taken into account.

Principally O'Casey employs emotions and "emotional effects" as an integral part of his writing:

> *I do not agree with those who would banish emotion from the theatre ..., for, to me, emotion burns within the veins of life. We all feel it in sorrow, in joy, in fear, in hate, at births, weddings, burials, and when we achieve things. .... I believe that all the arts should meet in the drama - architecture in the framework of the design, painting in the scenery, music in an occasional song and dance, and literature in a play's dialogue.* [14]

In *Juno and the Paycock* he makes use of various visual elements in several ways. When the play starts, Mary "... is arranging her hair before a tiny mirror perched on the table", wondering which ribbon to wear in her hair; the gay, green colour of the ribbon she chooses sharply contrasts with the grey atmosphere of the tenement house, where the Boyles live, and with her brother Johnny, whose "... face is pale and drawn ...", who has "... a tremulous look of indefinite fear in his eyes" and "... is sitting crouched beside the fire" when the curtain rises. Later on, the ribbon may be interpreted as an early sign of the superficial character of the relationship between Mary and Charles Bentham, a school-teacher, who distinguishes himself by carrying "... gloves and a walking-stick"[15], as Bentham leaves Mary and the child she is going to have. But the gay colour may also be considered a symbol of the hope that there is perhaps a way out of "tenement houses", a hope, which is also symbolized by the unborn child.

> MRS. BOYLE: *We'll go. Come, Mary, an' we'll never come back here agen. Let your father furrage for himself now; I've done all I could an' it was all no use - he'll be hopeless till the end of his days. I've got a little room in me sisther's where we'll stop till your trouble is over, an' then we'll work together for the sake of the baby.*
>
> MARY: *My poor little child that'll have no father!*
>
> MRS. BOYLE: *It'll have what's far betther - it'll have two mothers.*[16]

Whereas the women in the play generally represent all that stands for hope, the roles of the men underline the chaos of the situation. When the furniture men have removed the furniture which has not been paid for and which the Boyles had bought in anticipation of a legacy, they leave behind an empty stage, "... which stands there as a physical symbol of a disintegrating family and a disintegrating country", and

> *The Paycock himself makes the connection for us as he stumbles drunkenly about in search of the missing chairs: 'The counthry'll have to steady itself .... it's goin' ... to hell ... Where'r all ... the chairs ... gone to ... steady itself, Joxer ...' It is literally 'chassis' on the stage, a visual chaos symbolising the harsh truth that lies behind the comedy of the Paycock's speech: 'I'm telling you ... Joxer ... th' whole worl's ... in a terr...ible ... state o' ... chassis!' The symbolic implications give this scene its power, but they arise with perfect naturalness out of the plot: the arrival of the furniture men is simply the inevitable outcome of the action set in motion by the will.*[17]

It is evident that German translations of *Juno and the Paycock* have to consider the various and carefully worked-out relationships between symbols, dialogue and action in the play. The general criterion, which can be described as fidelity to the original, certainly also applies to translating dramas. In particular the translation of a play should reproduce the message and the medium of the original, which affords an effect similar to it.

Rendering a play from one language into another in such a way that the audiences in both countries have the same understanding and feeling of the play, implies several aspects, which are connected with forms and conditions of the reception of a work or its translation. Firstly, verbal and formal elements influencing the reception of a literary work have to be investigated. Then non-verbal conditions, such as the geographical, historical and cultural background of the country, in which an author wrote his work and to which he possibly refers directly or indirectly, must be analysed, and finally the interpretation of these conditions by the audience or by the author must be accounted for.

Most of the difficulties presented by works of literature in translating them are due to differences in time and in their historical or cultural backgrounds. In the case of *Juno and the Paycock*, however, the aspect "background" is particularly significant, for the action as well as verbal and formal elements of the play are intimately connected with specific historical and cultural conditions. Jules Koslow says:

> *... O'Casey, more than any other modern dramatist exploited the events of his own life, his surroundings and the people he knew and observed.*[18]

It should also be remembered that O'Casey wanted to show opinions in the theatre and regarded himself as a "political" playwright.[19]

Hence, according to the previous statements, the problems which arise when translating *Juno and the Paycock* can be divided into three main groups: problems associated with the historical background of the drama, connected with its language and form, and problems referring especially to cultural background.

The translator must not wait for these problems. The first sentence of the first stage direction illustrates the difficulties he is confronted with.

> *The living-room of a two-room tenancy occupied by the Boyle family in a tenement house in Dublin.* [20]

The "tenement houses", a familiar sight in Dublin, are houses which were built in the eighteenth century by wealthy people who later left them. Today they belong to the slum-district in the centre of Dublin, north of the River Liffey. In view of this stark contrast they can be considered as a symbol of social degradation.

German readers or a German audience will hardly understand the implications tied to the term and phenomenon "tenement houses", unless they are acquainted with the relevant aspects of Irish history.

Here, as in several other cases in this play, a short description of Irish history and an explanation of the main names, places or events mentioned in the drama, has to be given in the programme. Otherwise, many implications cannot be appreciated. The German performance of *Juno and the Paycock* in Kiel in 1972 made use of the possibilities a stage can offer: the action took place in a basement represented on the stage, thus indicating the social degradation of the Boyle family. Although it is possible to find a general term to substitute for the specific one, "tenement houses", this would mean that the specific environment, which constitutes the background of the message and which as a "microcosm" represents the "macrocosm" Ireland, or even the world, cannot be maintained.

The performance of *Juno and the Paycock* in Mainz in 1970 found a solution for illustrating the historical background; before the play began, a chronicle of events between 1922 and 1970 was projected onto the curtain.

The play refers to historical events in several ways. The action takes place during the months of September and November in 1922, i.e., during the "Irish Civil War", which broke out after the country had been divided in

1921 and the "Free State" established in 1922. The connection between historical events and *Juno and the Paycock* soon becomes apparent when the part Johnny plays in the drama is analysed.

Johnny participated in the "Easter Rising" in 1916, which has often been interpreted as the symbol of the Irish struggle for independence. Johnny also fought on the side of the Republicans against the "Free Staters" in O'Connell Street (July 1 - 5, 1922):

> MRS. BOYLE: *I don't know what's goin' to be done with him. The bullet he got in the hip in Easter Week was bad enough; but the bomb that shatthered his arm in the fight in O'Connell Street put the finishin' touch on him. I knew he was makin' a fool of himself. God knows I went down on me bended knees to him not to go agen the Free State.* [21]

He betrays his former comrade, the "Diehard" Robbie Tancred, who lives next door to the Boyle family. As a result he himself is killed by the "Irregulars".

In those days the Republicans were usually called "Diehards" or "Irregulars". An Irish or English audience is well acquainted with the meaning of these terms, but a German translation must illustrate them by additional information.

Not only the action, which is connected with Johnny, refers to historical conditions, problems of Trade Unionism and of the Labour Movement, which are based on personal experience and belong to the subjects, with which O'Casey occupied himself throughout his life, must also be considered when analysing the characters of Mary and her fiancé, Jerry Devine. The latter is described in the stage direction as a young man of "... about twenty-five, well set, active and earnest", and:

> *He is a type, becoming very common now in the Labour Movement, of a mind knowing enough to make the mass of his associates, who know less, a power, and too little to broaden that power for the benefit of all.* [22]

It must be kept in mind that Mary's thoughts have been affected by her acquaintance with books. The influence of literature, however, is at odds with the circumstances of her life. Her father once mentions some of the books Mary is interested in:

> BOYLE: *Aw, one o' Mary's; she's always readin' lately - nothin' but thrash, too. There's one I was lookin' at dh'other day: three stories, The Doll's House, Ghosts, an' The Wild Duck - buks only fit for chiselurs!*[23]

The implications of these plays by Henrik Ibsen are just as easy for a German audience to understand as they are for an English one. It is not difficult to realize either, that these sentences indirectly characterize Mary and the 'Captain' as well. Sometimes, however, several comments made by Boyle on the political situation or on the clergy in Ireland, for example, are not easy for Germans to grasp. This is unfortuante, as these comments are of great importance in that they help to characterize Boyle, and, moreover, they have the function of generalizing the historical implications, making *Juno and the Paycock* more than a mere political play. It is a drama of specific historical events which illustrate perennial problems.

The title of the play and the names of the characters provide no problems for a German version of *Juno and the Paycock*. A German audience is likely to understand the biblical implications given with the name Mary, or the possibility of a connection between "Devine" and the Latin word "divinus". The spectators would probably also realize that there might be a connection between the name of Charles Bentham and the utilitarian philosopher Jeremy Bentham. "Juno" refers to the name of the ancient Roman goddess, who, according to ancient mythology, was responsible for care of the home and marriage, and was always accompanied by peacocks. This symbol will be understood along with that of the "Paycock", the "miles gloriosus" and good-for-nothing, who in this play is "... struttin' about the town like a paycock with Joxer ..."[24], not caring for his family. Boyle's method of explaining his wife's name can also be readily employed in a German translation, although it must not be interpreted literally.

BOYLE: *... You see, Juno was born an' christened in June; I met her in June; we were married in June, an' Johnny was born in June, so wan day I says to her, 'You should ha' been called Juno,' an' the name stuck to her ever since.*[25]

But a German audience will scarcely realize that these persons are typically representative of "tenement house" occupants, and that their characterization is based on O'Casey's personal experience, - something which Saros Cowasjee analyses in *Sean O'Casey: The Man behind the Plays:*

> *... I did not fully comprehend how directly these two characters were drawn from life till I met Jimmy Boyle, son of Jack Boyle, and James Boyle, brother of Jack Boyle, in April 1958. ... James Boyle told me that O'Casey was once a great friend of theirs, and used to visit their two-room apartment in Gloucester Street, Dublin. It was here that he came across Jack Daly, the inseparable snug-mate of Jack Boyle. Jack Daly, who did not have as much as a sixpence to call his own, visited the Boyles' daily for a "cup o' tay." ... O'Casey, if he happened to be there, would sit near the fire listening to their talk, or writing something on bits of paper.*[26]

According to Cowasjee, Jack Boyle and Jack Daly even went in the company of a lawyer to see the performance of *Juno and the Paycock* with the intention of suing O'Casey for defamation.[27]

O'Casey introduced the idiom of the Dublin "tenement houses" into Irish drama as Synge before him had employed the speech rhythms of the dialects of the Aran Islander and the Wicklow peasant in his plays, and he formed his material into a poetic language, suffused with biblical overtones.

> *O'Casey's language gets its power from more than the idiom of the Dublin slums. It depends upon its witty distortions of syntax, its rhythm, repetition, dialect, malapropisms, alliteration, and a completely unrestricted vocabulary, one free to create havoc in any corner of the language, rather than restriced by the argot of a small group.*[28]

Of course, it is possible to find German equivalents for some of Joxer's "darlin" phrases or of Boyle's motto "I've a little spirit left in me still"; but the form of the language, shot through with quotations and references, selected from works by Burns, Macauley, Scott, Thomas Moore's *Melodies*, popular proverbs and Irish songs and ballads that an English-speaking audience is acquainted with, is almost impossible to translate into German. Hence there is nothing to do but to use "everyday language" maintaining as many implications and allusions as can be rendered without destroying the coherence of the play.

This confronts the translator with one of his cardinal problems. He must grasp the full significance of the allusion or implication in its cultural context and find a parallel within another context which produces the same effect. To do this he has a very useful tool in the form of the stage, which may be relied upon to give non-verbal support to the dialogue. Eileen O'Casey sees the main obstacle in a translation of her husband's work in its picturesque language. She believes it is necessary not only for a translator to be a poet, but for him to live in constant contact with the theatre.[29]

The difficulties in translating *Juno and the Paycock* culminate in the problem of maintaining its form. It is characterized by a juxtaposition of comic, tragic and melodramatic elements, along with music-hall songs and ballads. The action connected with Mary exhibits elements similar to those of the play *Maria Magdalena* by Friedrich Hebbel. A German audience is likely to understand these traits, and to appreciate the traditional aspects of the "legacy" theme. Although a German audience is acquainted with Shakespeare's dramas and, for instance a character like Falstaff, many performances of *Juno and the Paycock* in Germany have shown that the play has often been misinterpreted because the comic features of the play were exaggerated.[30] This resulted in the destruction of the relationship between language, form and content.

This paper could only deal with some of the problems, which arise when translating *Juno and the Paycock*. There are, of course, many more, which should be investigated in detail. Such a study would have to analyse the relationship between playwright, play, performances, reception and the translator of a work. This is accomplished with the assistance of several methods. First of all a translator must be informed on the current state of the philological research which has been done on "his" author and work. He must also be aware of the condition of the work's reception, which implies historical and sociological research. The form of the translation is determined to a great extent by its purpose, and here familiarity with the various translation theories and principles can prove advantageous. While translating, the translator must always keep in mind the potential reception of his work. This requires a thorough knowledge of his target audience. Finally, in the case of drama, the translator should also be intimately acquainted with the theatre and the dramatic methods and theories as well.

A method specifically for the translation of plays was developed by a team in the English Department at the University of Kiel and applied to the play *The Bloom of the Diamond Stone* by the contemporary Irish dramatist Wilson John Haire.[31] After a preliminary translation of the drama, a shortened version of the original was performed by students. Then the first translation was revised and performed on stage. The insights thus achieved, were fed back into the translation process before the final German version of *The Bloom of the Diamond Stone* was published. As there are several similarities between this play and *Juno and the Paycock*,[32] the experience gained by the project could be a major help in studying the problems of translating O'Casey's play. *Juno and the Paycock's* German reception need no longer remain in a "state o' chassis".

CHAPTER 11

Translation: Changing the Code: Soyinka's Ironic Aetiology

ANDRÉ LEFEVERE

Think in concentric circles: in the centre is the play that must be translated: the source text. Through its linguistic elements it belongs to the source language, and through that source language it partakes of the whole of the source culture. It also belongs to the source literature which has a code all its own, a repertory of literary procedures.

There are various possible strategies for translating this complex given. One may - and this has been the case until quite recently - consider the original play translated if one has managed to render the source text's linguistic circle into an acceptable target text. A step beyond this is the attempt to translate not only the linguistic circle but the cultural circle and the circle of literary procedures as well. This strategy seems currently in the ascendant and it probably comes closer to the ideal of an acceptable translation: the kind of translation that supplies its readers with the most numerous and soundest possible materials for the reception of the source text. But you can also take yet another step: you can try to influence either the linguistic circle (as in Browning's *Agamemnon*, e.g.) or the cultural circle and/or the literary circle towards change. Soyinka's *Bacchae* is an example of the latter strategy which tends to arise when the source text, the life of the author of the original, or both assume some kind of paradigmatic significance for the translator's own work, whether he happens to be what has traditionally been called "a writer in his own right" or a "mere translator" - for "only a writer is a translator, and whether translation constitutes the whole of his writing, or whether it is integrated into the rest of his work, he is that creator who could not be perceived by an idealization of creation".[1]

Soyinka unashamedly concentrates on the cultural and the literary circle: he admits in his "author's acknowledgement" that

> *a twenty-year rust on my acquaintanceship with classical Greek made it necessary for me to rely heavily on previous translations for this adaptation of* The Bacchae. *Two versions which deserve especial mention, in that I have not hesitated to borrow phrases and even lines from them, are those by Gilbert Murray . . . and William Arrowsmith.*[2]

Partisans of what used to be called "fidelity" in translation would presumably be rather shocked at this admission, but their presumed anger reveals itself totally irrelevant in the light of what Soyinka is trying to do, which brings us to one of the sore points of translation criticism. Even the recent past is still riddled with examples of the kind of "criticism" in which the critic simply establishes his own set of norms and then proceeds to damn the translator for each and every deviation he or she has made from those norms. A more fruitful exercise would be for the critic to try to establish the norms that have guided the translator, and then to criticize the translator for not having adhered to his own norms. In this way we would eventually arrive at a poetics of different translations and different schools of styles of translating which would be rather more valuable than a series of unexplicitated apodictic approaches to the phenomenon of translation.

What are the paradigmatic elements for Soyinka in Euripides' *Bacchae?* Euripides wrote his play in some kind of exile at the court of the king of Macedonia; Soyinka himself is no stranger to exile and various sorts of prosecution. "Euripides tends to mix together, or syncretize, the ecstatic cults".[3] Soyinka attempts syncretization in a much more comprehensive way. Euripides' *Bacchae* were written against the background of the last years of Peloponnesian War, which put an end to the colonial expansion of Athens. Soyinka's *Bacchae* are written against a background of post-colonial wars. The "theoi ksenikoi", the strange gods who "invaded" Athens "during the Peloponnesian War - probably as a result of the social stresses which it generated",[4] find their counterparts in the introduction of "strange gods" in Africa in the nineteenth and in Europe, North and South America in the twentieth century. In Euripides' time "the sophistic movement evinced a strong preoccupation with comparative ethnology and the collection of details about foreign lands and customs, partly with the intention of showing that "law" is a relative concept".[5] Soyinka writes in a similar climate of cultural relativism. Finally, both Euripides and Soyinka are concerned with the fate of the "near and distant dispossessed" (p. 7). Soyinka's dispossessed are emphatically made to include Africa and the third world in general, without excluding the dispossessed in the developed nations, witness the production note which states that "the slaves and the bacchantes should be as mixed a cast as is possible, testifying to their varied origins" (p. xiii).

But Soyinka also reinterprets the paradigm, and nowhere more obviously so than in the ending of the play. Not only does he reject "a total tragic vision, the doom of repetition, which the Western tragic concept or outlook from the Greeks right down to our present time entails"[6]; he is also dissatisfied with "the ending" of Euripides' *Bacchae*, especially "the petering off of ecstasy into a suggestion of a prelude to another play" (p. xi). In this he quite obviously overlooks that Euripides' ending is logically, though not obviously connected to the rest of the play, although the "detailed ... statement of the future fortunes of the surviving characters" is "to the modern reader very curious" indeed.[7] Yet it can be connected with the same aetiological tendency that manifests itself earlier in the play when Tiresias tries to explain why Dionysos was born from the thigh of Zeus, e.g.) and that also, in a more ironic guise, pervades Soyinka's own *Bacchae*. "Euripides seems to have been responding to a common aetiological taste that was particularly marked in the latter fifth century B.C. and had been accentuated both by the sophists and by the growth of local history."[8]

Soyinka's Shavian introduction to his *Bacchae* is the literary procedure through which he expresses his re-interpretation of the cultural circle most clearly. He points out that

> *Land, the primary economy and primary stimulant of communal labour, its mystery of seasonal fluctuation, dearth and bounty is the natural base of vegetation religions. Material (harvest) benefits which derived from land were identified with spiritual rewards. Where the ritual responsibility for land renewal lay with a small elite, the economic powers of such a minority*

> *were limitless. A religion which transferred its ritualism to communal participation and identified self-renewal with the truth of land-renewal and food production fed ... on a long repressed reality. (p. ix-x).*

This goes not so far beyond a rather more pointed restatement of the consensus of classical scholars, which holds that

> *Dionysos is a democratic god: he is accessible to all, not like Pythian Appollo through priestly intermediaries, but directly in his gift of wine and through membership of his thiasos. His worship probably made its original appeal mainly to people who had no citizen rights in the aristocratic "gentile state" and were excluded from the older cults associated with the great families.*[9]

Soyinka moves towards a more personal interpretation when he compares the yearly fertility rites to an "effort to stimulate growth," that

> *must have struck the oppressed groups as hardly different from the 'public deterrent' - public flogging, breaking on the wheel etc. etc. meted out to the mine-worker who had ruined a piece of machinery, attempted to forment unrest or reduced the week's profit in some other way. Both forms of imposed penance were designed to stimulate greater productivity. What the class-conscious myths of Dionysos achieved was to shift the privilege for the supply of scapegoats to the classes which had already monopolised all other privileges. The magic munificence of Nature requires both challenge and sacrifice in all nature renewal myths; Pentheus, the aristocrat, provides both in the highly seditious version by Euripides (p. x).*

The theme of syncretism is gradually introduced by means of statements like "the Dionysiac is present, of course, in varied degrees of spiritual intensity in all religions" (p. vii) and

> *the definitive attachment to a suitable deity - in this case Dionysos - was nothing more than the natural, historic process by which populist movements (religious or political) identify themselves with mythical heroes at critical moments of social upheaval. Myth is part wish-fulfilment through hero projections (p. viii).*

The theme is boldly stated when Soyinka evaluates Agave's behaviour at the end of the play as an "admission of her last, aberrant mind after the enormous psychic strain of wilful challenge (also a necessity for evoking maximum powers) this last in-gathering releases the reluctant beneficence of Nature" (p. xi). This statement is very closely paralleled and further explicated in what Soyinka has to say about Dionysos' Yoruba counterpart Ogun:

> *rupture is often one visage of the Ogun destructive-creative unity ... offences even against nature may in fact be part of the exaction by deeper nature from humanity of acts which alone can open up the deeper springs of man and bring about a constant rejuvenation of the human spirit ... Such acts of hubris compel the cosmos to delve deeper into its essence to meet the human challenge. Penance and retribution are not therefore aspects of punishment for crime but the first acts of a resumed awareness, and invocation of the principle of cosmic adjustment.*[10]

Soyinka constructs his *Bacchae* around precisely this principle, which is symbolized by Ogun, the "god of metals, creativity, the road, wine and war" (p. vi), who "is best understood in Hellenic values as a totality of the Dionysian, Apollonian and Promethean values ... Ogun stands for a transcendental, humane but rigidly restorative justice.[11] Dionysos' "thyrsus is physically and functionally paralleled by the *opa Ogun* borne by the male devotees of Ogun" (p. vi), which explains why the role of Euripides' Bacchantes is to a large extent taken over by male slaves in Soyinka's *Bacchae*.

The "principle of cosmic adjustment" operates on the three levels on which Yoruba culture is organized: the individual, the social and the cosmic. Throughout what follows it must be borne in mind that these three levels are interrelated, even if they are discussed separately here. Individual adjustment takes place in the case of each of the major human characters, even if they have to pay for it in terms of murder (Agave) and death (Pentheus). This adjustment also comes to Tiresias, who is transformed from "the type of mind which would harness to the cause of doctrinal conservatism the spontaneous emotional forces generated by a religious revival: he would not reject the new foreign cults ... but he would Hellenize and rationalize them"[12] into the Tiresias who can lyrically describe wine as

> *... the sun that comes after winter, the power*
> *That nudges earth awake. Dionysos comes alive in us.*
> *We soar, we fly, we shed the heavy clods of earth*
> *That weigh down the ethereal man*
> *To that first principle. Balance is the key (p. 30).*

No such similar transformation is obvious in Euripides.

The beginning of the play emphasizes social adjustment: the first scene takes place against a background of crucified slaves. The new religion will also bring political liberation. Also on the social level Dionysos will be acknowledged by his own family. On the cosmic level Dionysos is indeed *Phleus or Phleoos*, the abundance of life. His domain is, in Plutarch's words, the whole of the *hugra fusis* - not only the liquid fire in the grape, but the sap thrusting in a young tree, the blood pounding in the veins of a young animal, all the mysterious and uncontrollable tides that ebb and flow in the life of nature".[13] But Soyinka's Dionysos is more: "He has broken the barrier of age, the barrier of sex or slave and master" (p. 26). Through him "flesh is transcended" (p. 31). He is "the great joy of union with mother earth/And the end of separation between man and man" (p. 38). To resist Dionysos is therefore much more than - in purely Hellenic terms - "to repress the elemental in one's own nature; the punishment is the sudden complete collapse of the inward dykes when the elemental breaks through perforce and civilization vanishes".[14] In Soyinka's *Bacchae* both crime and punishment are rather different: the crime destroys the "mutual correspondence" between "the world of the unborn, the world of the dead and the world of the living"[15], which together make up the totality of man's world.

In the play crimes against Dionysos seem to be limited to the personal and social level, both mere symptoms of resistance on the cosmic level. Kadmos' decision to retire ("It is wrong to wait for death isn't it" (p. 24) and

Pentheus' political arguments which have a very familiar modern ring about them, from "I shall have order!" (p. 27) to "Thebes shall stop at nothing to preserve her good name/Faded with anarchy and indecency" (p. 29), the notion that "power/Is all that matters in the life of man" (p. 33) and the "duty to preserve/The territorial integrity of Thebes" against "alien monsters/Who have invaded Thebes" (p. 66). The punishment, on the other hand, takes on the character of grace: wine springs in red jets from the head of Pentheus, and everybody partakes in the final "communion rite" announced in the subtitle of the play.

Soyinka's Shavian introduction is followed by what is, in essence, a Shavian historical play, which also displays certain affinities with the historical re-interpretations both Max Frisch and especially Friedrich Dürrenmatt used to produce in the fifties and early sixties. The main mode is one of "ironic aetiology", which Euripides himself is not without in many of his own plays. The mode puts historical and/or mythological events or, in Soyinka's case, the whole of the original text at a distance and manipulates them in such a way that the spectator or reader is not only invited to share the playwright's interpretation of the material, but also prepared for often striking departures from that material which reflect the playwright's own vision. Yet this vision is never (as in Brecht's case) stated in very explicit ideological terms. Soyinka's contribution to the genre appears to be most significant in the revalorization of gestural, theatrical elements. His manipulation of the material does not limit itself to the verbal level. It also extends to the use of elements taken from other theatrical traditions. There is, e.g. the essentially music-hall scene, which is also reminiscent of the revue elements traditionally present in Yoruba folk opera, intended to rather obviously dramatize the point that Dionysos' thyrsus is, first and foremost, a fertility symbol. Kadmos shows Tiresias his latest contraption: "the first collapsible thyrsus in Attica" (p. 25). Said thyrsus keeps collapsing, a fact probably not unrelated to Kadmos' advanced years, and Tiresias finally advises him to "put it back in your trousers" (p. 26). Kadmos obliges, but not without observing that "I should have let the joiner show me how. But it could only make him cocky" (p. 26), at which the two old men exit, guffawing.

Similarly, Pentheus' absurdly limited state of mind is described by Dionysos in a speech reminiscent in style of the theatre of the absurd:

> *You, Pentheus, because you are a man of chains. You love chains. Have you uttered one phrase today that was not hyphenated by chains? You breathe chains, talk chains, eat chains, dream chains, think chains. Your world is bound in manacles. Even in repose you are a cow chewing the cud but for you it is molten iron issuing from the furnace of your so-called kingly will. It has replaced your umbilical cord and issues from this point..* (pp. 65 - 66).

Much of what the chorus says appears closer to the African praise song (Soyinka himself points out that "some lines in this version ... come from traditional praise-chants", p. vi) than to the traditional diction of the Greek chorus. And yet here too the affinity with Greek tragedy in its nascent state is greater than one would think at first sight: here too

> *the forms that have newly entered are not something the author has thought of by chance or invented freely; rather they are drawn into tragedy from the various realms of religion, the state, custom and morality. They are then filled with a particular action and as it were individualized.* [16]

It might similarly be argued that the scene in which the slave leader becomes possessed harks back to scenes of possession in the Engungun rituals, in which a man

> *becomes possessed, as we say by a spirit or a daemon; and in this state he works out his own salvation, as it were, while the audience of initiates is drawn through empathy with him into communion with the daemon, till they ultimately reach that state of ecstatic release which constitutes the objective of the ritual.* [17]

The playwright himself has, of course, no absolute control over the procedures in the repertory. Soyinka's *Bacchae* begins with a speech by Dionysos, just as Euripides' *Bacchae* does. This kind of Euripidean opening soliloquy is traditionally equivalent to an introduction of the setting and to what would in our theatres be conveyed in the form of programme notes. The effect of Soyinka's opening speech, however, is harder to assess against the background of a repertory that has come to include the Brechtian alienation device.

The liturgical procession (whose stasima again point to nascent Greek tragedy) with which the play opens is designed to dramatize several of the points made in the introduction. It is part of the old aristocratic religion, the fertility festivals in which a scapegoat - invariably a slave, which adds to the political tensions of the moment - is ritually flogged to death to symbolize the demise of the old year. Because of the volatile political situation Tiresias has taken the place of the slave.

Tiresias' outburst against the slaves who have been flogging him: "Can't you bastards ever tell the difference between ritual and reality" (p. 9) neatly dramatizes what has been written on page x of the introduction, just as his remark to Dionysos: "a priest is not much use without a following, and that's soon washed away in what social currents he fails to sense or foresee" (p. 11), dramatizes the argument advanced on page ix.

When Dionysos appears he breaks up the old liturgy, or rather makes those who are enacting it abandon their roles, priests and vestals alike, and the slave leader states both the social and cosmic dimensions of the play:

> *This master race, this much vaunted dragon spawn*
> *Have met their match. Nature has joined forces with us.*
> *Let them reckon now, not with mere men, not with*
> *The scapegoat bogey of a slave uprising*
> *But with a new remorseless order (pp. 7 - 8).*

The two scenes in which Dionysos shows the doomed Pentheus what his powers will be able to achieve in the future are rooted in another theatrical tradition, that of the mime often used, as here, to introduce other "times" or "places" into the body of the play in a very condensed form. The two scenes also serve to reinforce the theme of religious syncretism: in the first scene "a movement (of light?) turns our attention to the bust of Aphrodite. The face is coming off. Underneath, the mocking face of

Dionysos" (p. 67) and the scene ends with "a snap black-out, except on the altar of Aphronysos" (p. 68). In Euripides' *Bacchae* Pentheus also makes the connection between Aphrodite and Dionysos (lines 221 - 225), but in words only. In the second scene a Christ-like figure is seen changing water into wine, but "his halo is an ambiguous thorn-ivy crown of Dionysos" (p. 68).

Even where Soyinka does not directly quote from other theatrical traditions, he still emphasizes the gestural. Word and gesture are considered equivalent in Yoruba drama, both in the traditional Alarinjo theatre and in Yoruba folk opera. Soyinka uses gesture to convey his interpretation of Euripides' words to the spectator or reader.

This procedure can be observed most obviously in the translation of Euripides' interjection, "A" (line 810), often regarded as the turning point in the play, when Dionysos has finally made up his mind to punish Pentheus into "Dionysos is holding out a cup (the same as last seen) to Pentheus" (p. 69). The cup has been used in the mime-scenes interpolated to dramatize Dionysus' future power. Pentheus "slowly, dreamily, raises the cup to his lips" (p. 69) and we witness "the beginning of a psychic invasion, the entry of the god into his victim, who was also in the old belief his vehicle".[18]

Sometimes the gestural encompasses a whole scene, as in the possession scene culminating in orgasmic self-release, the scene in which Kadmos and Tiresias compare their clothes, the scene in which Dionysos begins to dress Pentheus in women's clothes, and the scene in which the slaves enact "a terse series of dramatic motions which takes its motif from the following invocation, the decisive gesture of throwing their lot with the Bacchantes, the casting off of the long vassalage in the House of Pentheus" (p. 79). The most theatrical of the gestural scenes is probably the one in which Dionysos' followers invoke the god and almost force him to bring about his own liberation.

Sometimes the gestural is confined to a slight detail, as when "an officer salutes and exits" (p. 27) after Pentheus gives the order to hunt down the

Bacchantes. Sometimes it consists of the introduction of a few more silent characters to underscore a point: when Dionysos is brought in, a captive, for his first confrontation with Pentheus, "three or four Bacchantes are with him, their hands similarly tied" (p. 39). The gestural also assumes the shape of a stage-effect, a contemporary equivalent of the Greek deus ex machina, through the use of light at the end of the play. There are precedents in antiquity: "any place (or person) struck by lightning was felt in antiquity to be uncanny, a point where the natural world had been touched by the supernatural"[19] and in Euripides' *Bacchae:* "again (when Pentheus is discovered), as when the divine voice was heard before, there is a supernatural increase of light. Then, the fire by Semele's tomb blazed up; now there is something like a flash of lightning, but one that seems more than momentary".[20] Soyinka transforms this into: "the theme music of Dionysos wells up and fills the stage with the god's presence as a powerful red glow shines suddenly as if from within the head of Pentheus, rendering it near-luminous. The stage is bathed in it instantly" (p. 97).

The gestural is sometimes combined with music, as in Dionysos' theme music described above and the music made by slaves and Bacchantes, but more often with words. A poignant example of this procedure is the ending, when Agave calls for a ladder to put Pentheus' head on the palace walls. The slave leader executes her command, she rushes up the ladder and puts the head where she wants it, whereas in Euripides' *Bacchae* she merely cradles the head in her arms in the scene of her madness. Similarly, while they are waiting for the news of Pentheus' death, slaves and Bacchantes enact "a stylised mime or the hunt. It ends just before the "coup de grace" at the entry of the officer" (p. 80) who then proceeds to tell his story. The most obvious example is the translation of Kadmos' "Ho mè patheis su, deuro sou stepsô kara/kissôi (lines 341 - 2, "Lest such be thy fate, let me crown thine head/With ivy" in the Loeb Classical Library translation)[21] as

> *Misjudging the thoughtful distant mood of Pentheus, he thinks he has at least mollified his stand. He removes the wreath from his own head.*
>
> KADMOS: *Here, take mine. Let me wreathe*
> *Your head with leaves of ivy (pp. 34 - 5).*

Switches in register also serve to bring Soyinka's interpretation of his original across. The most obvious switch is that from blank verse, usually reserved for those passages in which the influence of the god Dionysos is more obviously apparent, to prose. The scene in which Kadmos and Tiresias dress to go dancing for Dionysos provides several examples: Kadmos' "Thebes has fallen out of love with our fossilized past and needs to embrace a new vitality" (p. 23) is followed by his putting on his crown, saying "What do you think? Not too ... dashing is it", to which Tiresias replies "A bit fanciful for your age" (p. 23). The dialogue then modulates back to Tiresias' observation: "Pentheus doesn't know his own flesh. And when he does he'll think he's duty-bound to cut it out of himself" (p. 24), which is in turn followed by:

KADMOS: *Here's your crown. Trad or trendy?*

TIRESIAS: *We-e-e-ell, one is madness and two*
is fashion (p. 24).

The switch in register often modernizes and clarifies by means of amplific-ation. Euripides' "hos ekpuroutai lampasin kerauniais/sun metri, Dious hoti gamous epseusato" (244 - 5, Loeb: "Who, with his mother, was by lightning-flames/Blasted, because she lied of Zeus's love") is, e.g. trans-lated as

... a brat who got roasted
Right in his mother's womb, blasted by the bolts
Of Zeus! The slut! Slandered Zeus by proclaiming
The bastard's divine paternity. That myth he instantly
Exploded in her womb, a fiery warning against all profanity
(p. 28).

Similarly, Dionysos' terse "horôn horônta, kai didôsin orgia" (Euripides, 470 Loeb: "Nay, eye to eye his mysteries he bestowed") becomes:

DIONYSOS: *Will you reduce it all to a court*
of enquiry? A fact-finding commission such as
One might set up to decide the cause
Of a revolt in your salt-mines, or a slave-uprising?
(p. 41).

Sometimes the explanation becomes rather obvious, as when Tiresias tells "Kadmos, in Greek the name Pentheus signifies/Sorrow. Does that mean anything? Let's hope not" (p. 36), or when the herdsman likens the sleeping Bacchantes to "a scene just like a painting on a vase" (p. 58).

Verbal interpolations also play a structural part. Dionysos' "Monos su poleos tesd huperkamneis, monos/toigar s'agones anamenousin hous se chre" (Euripides, 963 - 4 Loeb: "Alone for Thebes thou travailest, thou alone/ Wherefore thee wait struggle and strain foredoomed") has to become

> *Yes, you alone*
> *Make sacrifices for your people, you alone.*
> *The role belongs to a king. Like those gods, who yearly*
> *Must be rent to spring anew, that also*
> *Is the fate of Heroes (p. 78).*

to prepare the spectator or reader for the communion rite at the end of the play. Similarly, the irony which is present in Euripides' *Bacchae* in the many references to Actaeon, another member of Kadmos' family who was torn apart limb from limb for offending the gods, is given added poignancy in Soyinka's play in that it is Pentheus himself who mentions the name: "The nearest fate I can devise to Actaeon's/Piecemeal death at the jaws of his hunting hounds" (p. 35).

Both gesture and language contribute to reinforce the impression of religious syncretism: a Maypole dance evolves when Agave whirls the thyrsus (p. 90), the Bacchantes' invocation has summoned Dionysos, very much in the way incantation is supposed to summon the power invoked in African religious practice: "You willed him,/Summoned him, your needs/Invoked his presence" (p. 54), and some of Dionysos' attributes are rather obviously Ogun's. It is Ogun who "made an anvil of the mountain-peaks/Hammered forth a thunderous will" (p. 21) who sees to it that "the fire is tamed in new greenery of life" (p. 21), and who has "limbs of mahogany" (p. 50).

Finally, both language and gesture are responsible for a certain Africanization of the Greek original, be it more obvious as in Tiresias' "Dionysos I presume" (p. 10) and the noise the Bacchantes make when Dionysos is chained, "a kind of ululating which is found among some African and Oriental peoples and signifies great distress, warning, or agitation" (p. 46), or more subtle as when "the holy hills of Ethiopia" (p. 18) are included in Dionysos' travels or when an African proverb surfaces in the officer's story: "You know that saying - a man the people seek/To roast rubs himself in oil, crouches beside an open fire/Moaning, I have a chill" (p. 85) - rather more vivid than the blindness Zeus used to smite his victims with in Greek antiquity.

I have tried to show how the three concentric circles can be translated, how a translation can be used to further change, both in cultural and literary terms, and how the repertory of literary procedures can be called upon to translate an author's intentions into a work of literature. I hope this analysis may be of some use in undermining two still powerful prejudices: that translations are somehow "not creative writing" and that they are hardly worthy of critical study. I hope to have highlighted the creativity that lies behind the present translation and I also hope to have shown that statements made in the course of a comparative analysis of source text and translation possess a much higher degree of intersubjective falsifiability than most of the statements usually made in critical or theoretical discourse. In short, translation allows both the writer to exercise his creative genius and the theorist to make statements which are scientifically testable to a high degree.

CHAPTER 12

The Synchronic Salome

MARILYN GADDIS ROSE

Arthur Symons is probably right when he has his poetic persona aver, "And always, when they dance, for their delight,/Always a man's head falls because of them."[1] This is the predictable mishap whenever Salome or Herodias encounters John the Baptist and Herod. The motif is so prevalent in painting, literature, and music of the French-oriented Decadence, 1870 - 1914, that it has to be considered a significant cultural phenomenon, a symptom before becoming a simple fad. The motif, of course, is notably diachronic also,[2] having many an explicit fatal avatar between 32 A.D. when, according to Josephus in *Jewish Antiquities* (93 - 94 A.D.), such a nymphet may indeed have danced for her platterfull and 1917, when Eliot's Prufrock ruefully remembers being a platterfull. Her repeated reappearances are puzzling, for we lack, quite frankly, evidence to support a neat conjecture that analogous cultural conditions set her vengeful veils in motion. If anything, our evidence suggests that there are no corresponding cultural connections between the medieval and Renaissance whirlwind enchantress of the benign nether world,[3] and the artistic corporealizations after Flaubert's *Salammbô* in 1863. Flaubert's writhing Carthaginian priestess was probably the artistic catalyst for Salome's reappearances during the Decadence of 1870 - 1914.[4] She impinged upon artistic consciousnesses at a time when there was a collusion of socio-economic expansion, artistic over-cultivation, and impending readjustments in Western male-female roles.

Socio-economically, an exhaustion of native markets and materials was sending the French into North Africa. The French went into Algeria in 1830; Empress Eugénie opened the Suez Canal in 1869; the French became increasingly influential in Tunisia, eventually having it as a protectorate by 1881; they intervened increasingly in Morocco before receiving it as a protectorate in 1912. Besides putting North Africa into the French popular press while putting French military and colonists into North Africa, this imperialism put North Africa and its Middle Eastern culture into the collective mind. There was greater ease of travel. Scholarship in Middle Eastern studies was boosted by this access to materials. There was a much greater flow of goods. In both the fine and decorative arts, the Middle East became fashionable. The taste of the Belle Epoque and the German Pompöse found the Middle East a source of piquant decorative additions. The expositions of 1855, 1867, 1878 and 1889 showed Parisians tasteful adaptations of Middle Eastern styles.

The adaptations were, above all, visual and plastic. Academy painters needed only to follow the Middle Eastern penchant of Ingres and Delacroix, until Moreau in his 1877 exhibition did for Salome what Doré had done for Dante, i.e., fixed the visualizations of the cultivated Westerner. Huysmans in *A rebours* (1884) describes two of Moreau's Salomes with sufficient exactitude to permit their reconstruction.[5] *A rebours*, which Symons in his book on Oscar Wilde calls a "Breviary of the Decadence,"[6] gave English Decadents support and inspiration. Wilde's *Dorian Gray* draws on it; Beardsley identified with its protagonist Des Esseintes.[7] Opera also exploited the visual appeal and cultural exoticism of the new terrain with Meyerbeer's *L'Africaine* (1865), Verdi's *Aïda* (1871), Gounod's *Le Tribut de Zamora* (1881) and Massenet's *Hérodiade* (1881). Salome herself was not always evil. In Massenet's opera, where she does not dance, she stabs herself when a jealous Hérode cannot stomach her blessed romance with Jean. Loïe Fuller's Dance of the Seven Veils at the Folies-bergère is described by Mallarmé as purifying motion.[8]

But Mallarmé's own Hérodiade is a vicious virgin responsible for Jean's head soaring to sainthood. For, the fin-de-siècle Salome is a complex masculine motif, not an unnatural choice for writers, bombarded with Middle Eastern accouterments and designs, and living in a time of subtle social readjustments. Huysmans metes out punishment directly to Des Esseintes for having used God's creatures as objects; Des Esseintes pays in broken health for his attempts to use animals, people, and his own body, as stimulus-producing goods. On the other hand, the Salome motif provides an opportunity for reassuring projection. Salome, whom Herod attempts to use as an object (i.e. she will dance on demand), retaliates by using a man as an object, but is punished for her presumption. On this score, if we may put it this way, no creators are more explicit than Oscar Wilde and Richard Strauss.

Wilde would not have had to be perverse to have seized upon this story. He was such an arbiter of fashion that he could have chosen the motif simply because, as we have just demonstrated, it was reaching fad proportions. Strauss was not perverse, but like Mallarmé he could admire the complexity and completeness of the motif as dramatic material - and unlike Mallarmé he had the patience and industry to finish his piece.[9]

Wilde and Strauss between them effect a synchronic tone poem with words and gesture. It is linguistically synchronic, for it was written in English with French words,[10] translated into German literally, but with a consistent selection of the most concise equivalents available, by Hedwig Lachmann.[11] It is artistically synchronic, for Strauss pruned, tightened, and rearranged the libretto to enhance, but not to replace, his program music dramatization.

To reach dramatic form, *Salome*, a brief one-act play to begin with, had to reduce its language, its verbal sign system, in short, and make manifest, while expanding - through costume, setting, blocking, gesture, and, above all, music - the referents of its sign system. Is it paradoxical that a play considered the epitome of Decadence had to lose its Decadent diction before it could survive in world repertory?

No, on the contrary, it proves the rule. Decadent diction is not well suited to dramatic performance. Minimally charged with semantic loads and syllabic sound associations, Decadent diction functions best when functioning lyrically.[12] I.e., it is best overheard in the inner ear of the reader's imagination. Even when we hear a poet or actor read poetry, we transpose the situation into an imaginary "real" one, e.g., Frost confronting snowy woods, Lamartine hearing again Elvire Charles lament against the lapping waters of Lake Bourget.

Lyrical language on stage can be tolerated only when it leaves to non-verbal signs the function of dramatic interaction and plot advancement. By itself it ushers in a moment of relative stasis, transferring the action of necessity to the spectator's inner stage as he visualizes the actor's references. *Romeo and Juliet* stops when the hero or heroine feels compelled to apostrophize; only when Shakespeare achieves dramatic poetry in, say, the later tragedies like *Lear* does the plot keep going, and even a play like *Lear* stops when the voice becomes lyrical - signalling events the dramatic action cannot make visible in front of the spectator. Molière in this connection only happens to use verse, and present-day spectators of Racine must remember that doom is in the wings. (Translators of Racine fail on stage unless like Robert Lowell or Tony Harrison they add references to bizarre acts of violence to the monologue repertory.[13]) Lyrical language on stage is an unqualified success only when of sufficient brevity, as it is, say, in Yeats's *Plays for Dancers*, for the spectator to internalize the play completely from the stylized cues of the ritualistic movements and spare harmonizing lines. Note "spare." Decadent writing never is. The Decadent's love-hate relationship with language made him overwrite, lured by sound, led astray by multiple associations, essentially distrustful of extensive semantic loads. Maeterlinck (and even a late-comer like Claudel) makes spectators feel, as Eliot says à propos of his own *Murder in the Cathedral*, meritorious and patiently bored.[14]

Salomé, as Wilde wrote it, is embarrassing, inducing at best amusement and chargin. It really cannot be proved that we have in Lachmann's translation a decided improvement over either Wilde's French or English (on the kabbalistic assumption that each is transcribing an Ur-Salome text). Both French and German have an advantage here in customary formal and familiar second persons; the "thee, thy, thou" of the English version probably sounded odd in the late nineties; they sound exceptionally silly today. It happens also that at the critical moment when Salome demands Jokanaan's decapitated head, Lachmann can subtly understate by translating "ce que" and "ce qui" as "was" while the English transcription "the thing that" overstates:

> *Dites aux soldats qu'ils descendent et m'apportent ce que je demande, ce que le tétrarque m'a promis, ce qui m'appartient.*
>
> *Geh zu den Soldaten, heisse sie hinabsteigen und mir bringen,*

> *was ich verlange, was der Tetrarch mir versprochen,*
> *was mein ist.*
>
> *Go to the soldiers and bid them go down and bring me*
> *the thing I ask, the thing the Tetrarch has promised me,*
> *the thing that is mine.* [15]

However, what made *Salome* successful at the Kleines Theatre, Berlin, November 15, 1902, was the total theatricality of the production of Friedrich Kayssler and Hans Oberländer working under Max Reinhardt. This total spectacle, which included specially commissioned incidental music by Max Marshalk and Friedrich Bermann, partially transferred the dramatic movement to the non-verbal and, of course, relied on the overall affectivity which the legend had accrued from prior fin-de-siècle portrayals.

This was the production Strauss saw. For his opera which had its premiere, December 9, 1905, he used both the Lachmann translation and Wilde's French original.[16] To construct a dramatic tone poem for which music and text are mutual commentaries, complementing pose and dance, Strauss generally made minor abridgements, not even letting the vocalists repeat lines for comprehension and emphasis. Strauss responds both to audience anticipation and musical pacing by introducing Iochanaan's voice after 18 speeches (instead of after 35 as in the play) and by bringing Salome on stage after 38 speeches (instead of after 67 as in the play). Narraboth, the guards' captain whom Salome can seduce simply by calling him by name, is named from the outset. A verbal seduction of this sort is probably too subtle for stage in any event; the seduction can be represented better by orchestration. Syntax emphasis, indeed logical emphasis, is subordinated to the melodic and orchestration needs of onomatopoeic music.[17] The libretto is a *mere* verbal component of the total poem. The libretto contains prompting cues, frequently submerged by the orchestra.

As a one-act play, *Salomé* can be read and analyzed (i.e., transcribed to the reader's inner stage) as a compact three-act "well-made" play. So read, it starts out quietly and builds on the point of expected clash and dénouement. (The legend itself, as abumbrated by fin-de-siècle treatments is the background, so no exposition is needed.) However, it is obvious from the surging Schopenhauerian orchestration as the curtain opens, from the tempo, volume, pitch, and vocalized urgency that we are beginning with the climax. When Iochanaan rises from the courtyard cistern at Salome's command, as listener/spectators we are made to admire an adroit analogue of prematurely terminated intercourse. We expect the dissatisfied partner (Salome) to seek satisfaction. Subsequent orchestration and vocal interchange maintain the tempo, volume, and pitch of urgency. Strauss, while keeping close to Wilde, can make use of vocal counterpoint and accelerate the plot development. (Counterpoint is virtually unavailable to a dramatist). Salome's dance, disparaged by Norman del Mar as a Viennese waltz,[18] but sounding like an elaborate vaudeville adagio to a less-trained ear, represents more than her part of the bargain with Herodes. It is her means of keeping undiminished her own sexual excitement after Iochanaan climbs down into the cistern. When the execution has taken place, her request, quoted earlier, is enunciated rapidly in an ascending scale, deemphasizing further the actual words. The head, now an object of limited use, appears as manipulated by the executioner's arm, an eerie recapitulation of the earlier scene when Iochanaan rose by his own power. Yet her self-hypnosis prevails for a completion of her act of ardor in full stage view. The music at this point would be equally suitable for a technicolor tragedy of Hapsburg Vienna (a remake of *Mayerling*, for example) We have subsiding volume and tempo imitating the tranquility of passion spent, when Herodes abruptly has Salome killed in full stage view.

As a dramatized masculine motif, Salome is indeed nearly unendurable and both motif and namesake must be brought conclusively to an end. "Tuez cette Femme!" orders Hérode (p. 80); "Kill that woman!" orders Herod (p. 347). But Lachmann realizes that the situation is more general: "Tötet das Weib!" (p. 56) and leaves to Strauss the distancing of the episode in history: "Man tötet dieses Weib!"[19]

Salome poses a general threat, but even though the Louvre Moreau exhibition in 1961 initiated a recrudescence of Art Nouveau, it did not, we notice, inspire any new Salomes, except in continuing repertory. Perhaps the motif will not emerge again until it acquires another cultural valence. Nor can it, we predict, ever again be staged with Decadent diction. The synchronic Salome is a hybrid art form, for Decadent drama cannot carry the crux of drama with dialogue alone.

CHAPTER 13

Translating Literature/Translated Literature: The State of the Art

ANDRÉ LEFEVERE

For a long time the study of translation has meant little more than the study of translating. How should one translate? How does one train good translators? Until the beginning of the twentieth century this type of translation study centred mainly on literary texts. It tried to answer a certain type of question related to what might be called "stylistic aesthetics" (How "good", how "apt" is a language at expressing what it expresses, what does it lose in translation?) and to the "genius" of languages and literatures (Why is literature X so much "better" than literature Y?). It also dabbled in linguistic philosophy and in linguistic psychology, producing many an analysis of "A as translator of B", in which a few memorable things might be said about either A, or B, or both, but not too many about translation.

Linguists would have us believe that modern linguistics has changed all that. The questions asked above, so delicisously speculative in nature and thus admitting of endless speculation, are still being answered to the present day. They are no longer central questions in the study of literary translation, which is shifting more and more from the study of translating literature to the study of how translated literature functions inside the system of a given native literature, thus effectively establishing a long postulated link with comparative literature.

The advent of a mainly linguistically inspired analysis of translating has contributed to the exclusion of the study of translating/translated literature from translation studies as a whole. It was considered that literary texts were too complex for the type of analysis based on linguistics. Alternatively, the specificity of literary translation could not be analysed by means of modern linguistics. This exclusion, elegant or not, of the study of translating/translated literature was also undertaken for practical reasons, especially in the late fifties when the impending triumph of machine translation necessitated the construction of relatively simple programmes that could be fed into machines. Now that the machine translation euphoria has subsided, there appears to be less reason to exclude more "complex" texts from the construction of such a programme. Consequently the latest development in modern linguistics, text linguistics, tries to make statements about both literary and non-literary texts. To a student of literature, however, some statements about literary texts sound suspiciously trivial, because they are dressed up in the garb of extremely complicated and unnecessary formalisation. But the important new phonomenon is that the dividing line seems to be disappearing. The rare pronouncements textlinguistics has seen fit to devote to the study of translation try to encompass all kinds of translated texts.

It would be wrong to write off most, if not all, of the results of about fifty years of translation study undertaken mainly from the linguistic point of view as "irrelevant" for the study of translating/translated literature. Literary scholars who are interested in the phenomenon of translated literature could use some of the instrumentation developed by linguistic translation analysis. By doing this they would render their own statements on translated literature less vague and less subjective. It might also help to standardise the language of translation studies as a whole.

Linguistic definitions of translation tend no longer to be normative. The old translation should render the information that is available in the source text into an acceptable text in the target language, preferably by using features in the target language equivalent to features used in the source text. This, however, has proven to be untenable. Instead translation is seen as a text which shows certain correspondences with the original and also certain deviations from it. The ideal of optimal translation is thus being tacitly abandoned. A distinction is made between the informational function of a translation and the linguistic features used to achieve this informational function. This distinction admits that the informational content remains invariant (or as nearly invariant as possible), whereas the form in which the information is "processed", so to speak, can change considerably. Moreover during the last ten years linguistics has devoted more and more attention to the pragmatics of the text, and the ways in which pragmatic features (what the old philologies used to call "realia", and what is still called by that name in Soviet and East European translation studies) are transposed from source text into target text. All in all, a much more flexible definition of translation has emerged, which could be formulated as follows. Translation is the result of an activity which derives from a text in the source language to a text in the target language which corresponds with the text in the source language in certain relevant features and can be substituted for it under certain circumstances. This type of definition is also, in practice, applied to texts on the basis of the concept of "family resemblances", i.e. not all features of the definition of translation need occur in a given text for that text to be treated or identified as a translation.

Seen from this angle, the concept of equivalence,[1] launched in the mid-sixties, has also lost much of its stringency. Some linguists propose abolishing it altogether. Others would tend to relativise it to a great extent. They would point out that other correspondences are also possible between source text and target text and that equivalence is not the only type of correspondence. They would further advocate restricting its use to the level of conceptual meaning only, or else to use it merely to denote the arbitrary permutability of texts on the basis of an intuitively accepted "identity" which would be semantic or pragmatic in nature. Adequacy seems, as a concept for use in translation studies, to have a brighter future than equivalence.

Deviations from the source text tend to be called "shifts" more and more, and a distinction is made between substantial and formal shifts. Substantial shifts have to do with the semantics, the communicative value of the source text. They often result in modulations, e.g. from general to particular, or from abstract to concrete, or from cause to effect. The result of modulation is often either an "explicitation" (the translator "explains" what is explicit in the source text) or a levelling of the source text (the translator reduces stylistic differences). Formal shifts are of less fundamental importance. Obligatory shifts are made necessary by the very difference in languages, but optional shifts are of great interest to the student of translated literature. They depend on the translator only, who may use them as stylistic features in order to influence the text he is producing, depending on whether the shifts his work shows have been motivated or unmotivated.

Much of the "realignment" in linguistic thinking about the phenomenon of translation has been caused by the move, which took place in linguistics at the end of the sixties, "beyond the sentence".[2] Texts were seen as the basic units of communication, and it was soon admitted that texts were inextricably bound up with contexts. This kind of statement many a rhetorician in imperial Rome or even many a sophist in Socratic Greece would have put aside as trivial. Still, it became generally accepted that generating texts was not just a matter of linguistic conventions only, but of linguistic and other semiotic conventions, mainly socio-cultural ones. It was even posited that aesthetic and moral constraints dominate all others during the process of text generation, with the proviso that structural-expressive constraints dominate cultural-semantic ones. They in their turn dominate structural-syntactic constraints. Effectively the discovery of text and context has freed the linguistic study of translation from its fixation on word and/or sentence and has enabled it to take many other factors into account. It has, of course, also greatly complicated its task.

In attempting to deal with these new complications, attempts to make the pragmatics of texts more manageable by drawing up typologies of texts have been disappointing. The old bipolar opposition literary-non-literary tends to surface again, and it is often overlooked that the cultural focus through which the reader approaches the text decides on its being literary or not. For it is not the actual features of the text which decide whether it is literary or not, but the way the reader relates to it.

On the other hand, pragmatics has influenced semantics to the extent that a typology of meanings has emerged, which is much more operational than the abortive typology of texts. Distinctions are made (and could profitably be made by students of translated literature) between

(a) conceptual meaning, in which the identity of Semantic Representation as opposed to the difference in semantic expression makes possible the transfer of meaning from source text to target text;

(b) stylistic meaning, which also says something about the relationship between the participants in a text; and

(c) the way the speaker /hearer sees himself playing his part, or establishes himself inside the cultural conventions regulating a text.

It is important then to make a distinction between stylistic category, being the social meaning expressed, and stylistic function, being the phonological, syntactic or semantic way in which that category is expressed. The former remains relatively invariant in different languages, the latter does not. Associative meaning consists of connotative, affective, collocative variants of meaning, and thematic meaning contains certain elements of sentences (for example, it is "responsible" for the difference between active and passive sentences).

Linguistic models[3] of the translation process have also not tended to be very successful. They have been either too vague or too inapplicable. These models should explain how a text came into being (not a sentence), on what linguistic, contextual and intertextual basis, and why each particular translation realises only one possibility among many. It would therefore seem more profitable to operate with a certain concept of "norm"[4], which is looser than that of "model". One would distinguish between the following norms[5]:

1. Preliminary norms: the translator asks himself what kind of a translation he wants to produce.

2. Initial norms: the translator decides on whether to adopt the code of the source text or that of the target text.

3. Operational norms: the translator makes use of the linguistic, contextual and intertextual instrumentation described above.

The area in which research done in contemporary linguistics tends to overlap most with the traditional research done in the study of literature is that of "text processing". In textlinguistics the concept can be said to cover all operations by means of which texts are derived from other texts. It is plain to see that both translated literature and all intertextual components of literary works may be subsumed under this concept as well.

It would be advisable though, for the study of translating/translated literature to abandon its own definitions of what a translation "ought" to be, and to accept the definition(s) proposed by linguistics in more recent years.[6] Past literature oriented theories of translation have rather uniformly and depressingly tended to be normative in outlook.[7] That is, they have been written mostly to justify a certain kind of practice and a certain manner of translating. Moreover, they have often been based on one kind of literary text (for example, the Bible). And they have been widened to include other texts in a manner not always warranted.

It could be argued that normative theories of translating literature have been formulated for so long because translated literature has always been the Achilles heel of a certain concept of comparative literature. One could not do without translations, but on the other hand one did not feel too inclined to admit this. Hence the desire to "ensure" the "best possible" translations, which, in practice, meant that the standards defining the "best possible" tended to change about every twenty years or so. It would seem most appropriate to avoid the continuation of this rather sterile succession of post-factum ukases and to banish the giving of rules for translating literature from the scientific study of translated literature altogether. This does not mean that from now on "anything goes" in the production of translations of literature. It does mean, however, that the giving of rules is limited to a field called "praxiology" or "didactics", and not seen as the central, and eternally unproductive problem a theory of literary translation has to solve.

If we accept that the definition of translation should not be determined by a certain practice limited to a certain place and time (even though each of these definitions have taken great pains to pass themselves off as "eternal" or "unchangeable"), we can look at the role translated literary texts play inside the literary system of a given language. We could widen the scope even more, if we looked at all the different kinds of "processing" which a given text is subjected to in the receiving literary and cultural system. In doing this we would consider what place it is given in handbooks of (world) literature written in the target culture, e.g., in what manner it is summarized, what "image" of it arises in the receiving culture, how this image changes, etc..

Translated literature is the channel through which most interliterary communication passes, or even has to pass. It is therefore of great importance that one should ascertain who translates, and with what goal in mind. To put it in "linguistic" terms, one should pay due attention to the "preliminary" and "initial" norms certain translators, or version writers, or imitators select.

Roughly speaking, we can distinguish between two kinds of translators, those who wish to influence the evolution of their native literature and those who do not, or do not primarily have that wish. In order to make this clear, it seems advisable to introduce here the notion of "polysystem"[8] for the description of a given literature.

The polysystem can be described as a canonised system, which is the leading "fashion" of a given day. It is vindicated and defended by a number of writers and critics and is taught as "the" literary standard to emulate in schools. In addition it influences the writing of "timeless" handbooks of poetics by its proponents. The polysystem also contains countercurrents, which try to displace the canonised system and replace it.

In this struggle between the canonised and the non-canonised systems, text processing plays an important part. Both canonised and non-canonised concepts of literature will look outside their own literature for support for their own claims. They will look for foreign models made available by text processing, and first and foremost by translation. If translators of literature want to promote either the canonised or the non-canonised concept, their choice of primary and initial norms, which dictates their choice of shifts and of processing contextual and pragmatic factors, is likely to be radically different.

Foreign "models" need not be limited to the literary domain. New philosophical, sociological and other doctrines, in so far as they are expressed in works of literature, will also make an impact on the target culture, without necessarily affecting the balance between canonised and non-canonised inside the literary polysystem.

Let us, for the sake of argument, call those translators who want their translations to take part in the struggle between canonised and non-canonised systems, "literary translators" pure and simple. Yet there are also those translators who do not, as "literary translators" do, limit their endeavours to the defense or advancement of a certain "poetic concept", i.e. a number of rules, a literary "fashion" on which either the canonised or the non-canonised systems are built. These translators are concerned not with changing and, eventually, ephemeral (even though they sometimes last two hundred years in Western literature) poetic concepts, but with "poetics" themselves. They want to show how a literary polysystem evolves, how it changes, what factors make it behave the way it does etc.. They are also concerned with the interaction between different literary polysystems. Part of their work may be taken up with the production of translations of literary works which are not intended to function as models, manifestoes, or calls to arms, but simply as information. Those translators might be called "metaliterary" translators, because their choice of initial and preliminary norms, as well as the shifts their work will show, will be based on insights gained from the scientific study of literature, not on critical convictions. It will also be clear that the divisions between both types of translations produced by both types of translators may run rather deep, while the metaliterary translator can never completely escape from the literary taste of his own time. It would, therefore, not be unwise for the study of translated literature to spend some time trying to ascertain what the initial and preliminary norms are a certain translator has selected, and why.

Whether linguistically oriented or not, the study of translated dramatic literature has been treated extremely superficially by translation studies.[9] It is easy to see that a linguistics which had not discovered the central notion of pragmatics could not devote too much energy to one of the most important aspects of drama, whereas literary analyses of translated dramatic texts very often were confined to its textual dimension, to what was on the page. Neither discipline developed the necessary tools to deal with other dimensions in a satisfactory way.

It would seem, for reasons described above, that the study of translated dramatic literature would do well to eschew all normative pretensions. It might productively concentrate on two main fields:

(a) the pragmatics of production, in which the way

a play is produced can also be seen as
a type of text processing, and

(b) the way in which certain productions influence the target dramatic literature.

Next to these two fields, there will also always be a need for the production of "metaliterary" translations of dramatic literary texts.

Finally, what is it all good for? We shall not, as a result of the "state" which the "art" has attained at this moment, be able to say what "good" translations are and what not, or how "good" translators should be trained and how not. What we shall be able to do, however, is to show how literature operates, through the study of translated literature, and we shall be able to do so without recourse to speculation, criticism or propaganda. In other words: the study of translated literature will be one of the angles from which light may be shed on the study of human communication in general, whereas the study of translating literature would represent only the description of one, usually short lived, attempt to influence that communication in a certain way.

For a selected and (minimally) annotated bibliography see the NOTES to this chapter, pp. 171-177.

Notes to Text

CHAPTER 1. VERBAL AND NON-VERBAL COMMUNICATION: DRAMA AS TRANSLATION.

1 Eric Bentley, *In Search of Theater* (New York: Vintage Books, Random House, 1953), p. 78.

2 John Kershaw, *The Present Stage: New Directions in Theatre Today* (London: Collins, 1966), p. 61.

3 Marjorie L. Hoover, *Meyerhold: The Art of Conscious Theater* (Amherst: University of Massachusetts Press, 1974), p. 66.

4 Lee Simonson, "The Ideas of Adolphe Appia" in Eric Bentley (ed.), *The Theory of the Modern Stage: An Introduction to Modern Theatre and Drama* (Harmondsworth: Penguin, 1968), pp. 27-50.

5 Ibid., p. 44

6 Ibid., p. 47

CHAPTER 2. *ROOTED* IN DIFFERENT PLACES.

1 Kalem, "Aussie Absurdist", *Time*, (New York, 14.2.1972), p. 55.

2 Elliot Norton, "'Rooted' a Lovely Play", *Boston Record American* (Boston, 26.1.1972).

3 Martin Gottfried, "Theatre", *Women's Wear Daily* (New York, 14.1.1972).

4 William Glover, "Down Under Drama", *Associated Press* (New York, 24.1.1972).

5 Kalem, p. 55.

CHAPTER 5. TRANSCENDING CULTURE: A CANTONESE TRANSLATION AND PRODUCTION OF O'NEILL'S *LONG DAY'S JOURNEY INTO NIGHT*.

1 Lionel Trilling, *Beyond Culture*, (London: Peregrine Books, 1965), p. 11.

2 For an excellent detail study of O'Neill's New England Irish Catholic background to this play (to which I am deeply indebted), see John Henry Raleigh, "O'Neill's *Long Day's Journey into Night* and New England Irish Catholicism" in Travis Bogard and William Oliver (eds.), *Modern Drama* (New York: Oxford University Press, 1965).

3 Henry Gifford, *Comparative Literature* (London: Routledge and Kegan Paul, 1969), p. 28.

CHAPTER 5.

4 Ibid., p. 29

5 Trilling, p. 12

6 Quoted in Gifford, p. 48.

7 Quoted in Olga Lang, *Pa Chin and His Writings* (Cambridge, Mass.: Harvard University Press, 1967), p. 70.

8 Ibid.,

9 Ts'ao Yu, *Family* (c. 1937 - 1945) - a dramatization of Pa Chin's novel, *Family*. (Unpublished translation by Jane Lai), Act III, Scene 2.

10 Ibid., Act II, Scene 3.

11 Eugene O'Neill, *Long Day's Journey Into Night* (New Haven: Yale University Press, 1955), p. 154.

12 Timo Tiusanen, *O'Neill's Scenic Images* (Princeton, New Jersey: Princeton University Press, 1968). In his study of the visual and aural elements of O'Neill's plays Tiusanen also comes to the conclusion that in *Long Day's Journey* O'Neill eschews his usual fascination with gimmicks like masks, etc. and relies almost entirely on words for his scenic images.

13 O'Neill, p. 176.

14 Ibid., p. 131

15 Travis Bogard, *Contour in Time* (New York: Oxford University Press, 1972), p. 427.

CHAPTER 6. AUDIENCE AIDS FOR NON-LITERARY ALLUSIONS? OBSERVATIONS OF THE TRANSPOSITION OF ESSENTIAL TECHNICALITIES IN THE SEA PLAYS OF EUGENE O'NEILL.

1 Eugene O'Neill, *Seven Plays of the Sea* (New York: Random House, Vintage Books 856, 1919).

2 Robert F. Whitman, "O'Neill's Search for a 'Language of the Theatre'," *Quarterly Journal of Speech*, 1960, XV1/2, pp. 154-170.

3 Doris Alexander, *The Tempering of Eugene O'Neill* (New York: Harcourt, Brace & World Inc., 1962).

4 Croswell Bowen, *The Curse of the Misbegotten* ..... (New York: McGraw-Hill, 1959), p. 64.

CHAPTER 6.

5 Liisa Dahl, *Linguistic Features of the Stream-of-Consciousness Techniques of ... Eugene O'Neill* (Turku: U.B., 1-70), p. 19.

6 *New York Herald Tribune*, New York, 16.11.1924, quoted in Barrett Harper Clark, *Eugene O'Neill* (New York: Robert M. McBride & Co., 1926), pp. 64-65.

7 Letter to Barret H. Clark in May 1919, quoted in Clark, pp. 41, 43.

8 John Masefield, *Salt-Water Ballads* (London: Elkin Mathews, 1913), p. 40.

9 Clark, p. 43.

10 O'Neill, pp. 58-59.

11 Clark, p. 44.

12 Egil Törnqvist, "Personal Nomenclature in the Plays of O'Neill", *Modern Drama* 8/1966, pp. 362-373.

U. Halfmann, "Zur Symbolik der Personennamen in den Dramen O'Neills", *Archiv für das Studium der neueren Sprachen und Literaturen* 121/206, pp. 38-45.

13 Jordan Yale Miller, *Eugene O'Neill and the American Critic* (Hamden - London: Archon Books, 1962), pp. 12, 77.

14 Arthur and Barbara Gelb, *O'Neill* (New York: Harper & Bros., 1962), p. 760.

CHAPTER 7. HAZARDS OF ADAPTATION: ANOUILH'S *ANTIGONE* IN ENGLISH.

1 It is only in the text published by Samuel French that this is deleted; it is kept in the Random House edition.

2 *The Nation*, 162 (March 2, 1946), p. 269.

3 *New Republic*, 114 (March 4, 1946), pp. 317-18.

4 *The New Statesman and Nation*, 37 (February 19, 1949), pp. 178-79.

5 Reprinted as "A Note by the Adapter", prefacing the Samuel French edition.

CHAPTER 8. PROBLEMS OF PROPRIETY AND AUTHENTICITY IN TRANSLATING MODERN DRAMA.

1 The major works in this field are listed in the bibliographies of the following books:

Reuben A. Brower, *On Translation* (New York: Oxford University Press, 1966).

Jirí Levý, *Die Literarische Übersetzung* (Frankfurt: Athenäum-Verlag, 1969).

Henri van Hoof, *Internationale Bibliographie von Übersetzungen - International Bibliography of Translation* (München: Verlag Dokumentation, 1973).

George Steiner, *After Babel* (London: Oxford University Press, 1975).

André Lefevere, *Translating Literature: The German Tradition from Luther to Rosenzweig* (Assen/Amsterdam: Van Gorcum, 1977).

Wolfram Wilss, *Übersetzungswissenschaft. Probleme und Methoden.* (Stuttgart: Ernst Klett, 1977).

2 Urteil des Landesgerichtes Berlin, 26.6.74., p. 2 (translated).

CHAPTER 9. HENRIK IBSEN IN ENGLISH TRANSLATION.

1 Robert Farquharson Sharp, *Peer Gynt* (London: Everyman's Library, 1921).

2 Michael Meyer, *Peer Gynt* (London: Methuen, 1973). First published by Rupert Hart-Davis (1963). The translation was commissioned by the Old Vic. Theatre Trust and performed in London in 1962.

3 Every Norwegian quotation is followed by my own literal English translation, a word for word rendering for the sole purpose of making the original text available. The Norwegian text is from *Ibsens Samlede Verker*, Bind I-III, Fakkelserien, (Oslo: Gyldendal Norske Forlag, 1962). These are the complete Works in 3 vols.

4 Literally: "everywhere to show up as a display poster for the Master's meaning".

5 William Archer, *Ibsen, Collected Works* (London: William Heinemann, 1902).

CHAPTER 9.

6 Una Ellis-Fermor, *Hedda Gabler and Other Plays* (Harmondsworth: Penguin Classics, 1973). First published under the title *Three Plays.* (1950). See Introduction, p. 21.

7 Ibid., p. 7.

8 Rolf Fjelde, *Four Major Plays* (New York: Signet Classics, 1965).

9 James McFarlane, *Ibsen Plays* (London: Oxford University Press, 1971).

10 The Norwegian line is "Farvel, frue" (Good-bye, Madam).

11 Peter Watts, *Ibsen. Ghosts and Other Plays* (Harmondsworth: Penguin Classics, 1975).

12 Miss Tesman calls Hedda "De" once, just before she leaves for the last time in Act IV.

13 Eva Le Gallienne, *Hedda Gabler and Other Plays* (London: Everyman's Library, 1966).

CHAPTER 10. PROBLEMS IN TRANSLATING SEAN O'CASEY'S DRAMA *JUNO AND THE PAYCOCK* INTO GERMAN.

1 See Heinz Kosok, *Sean O'Casey: Das dramatische Werk* (Berlin: Erich Schmidt Verlag, 1972), pp. 14, 45.

2 At the Abbey Theatre plays usually ran a week before the next play opened. See the following statements: David Krause, *Sean O'Casey and His World* (London: Thames and Hudson, 1976), pp. 17-31, and 110. David Krause, *Sean O'Casey: The Man and His Work* (New York: Macmillan, 1960), pp. 36-45. H. Kosok describes the form of repertoires at the *repertory theatres,* to which the Abbey belongs. See Heinz Kosok, "Die Anfänge der modernen Repertoire-Theaterbewegung in England and Schottland:, *Maske und Kothurn,* 3/4 (1968), pp. 318-340.

3 Sean O'Casey, *Two Plays: The Shadow of a Gunman and Juno and the Paycock* (London: Macmillan, 1925). See the letter of the publisher Daniel Macmillan to James Stephens in: *The Letters of Sean O'Casey* 1910-1941, ed. David Krause, I (London: Cassell, 1975), pp. 14-15.

4 See Klaus Völker, *Irisches Theater II: Sean O'Casey.* Dramatiker des Welttheaters dtv 6855 (2nd rev., ed., Velber, 1972), p. 114.

CHAPTER 10.

5 See e.g. Edward Hatim Mikhail, *Sean O'Casey: A Bibliography of Criticism.* With an introduction by Ronald Ayling (London and Basingstoke, 1972).

6 See Manfred Pauli, *Sean O'Casey: Drama-Poesie-Wirklichkeit* (East-Berlin: Henschelverlag, 1977), p. 251.

7 See Gert Otmar Leutner, "Umgang mit Sean O'Casey", *Theater Heute, IV,* 8 (1963), p. 17.

8 See Klaus Völker, p. 92 - The following statements refer to letters received from the "Kurt Desch Theater-Verlag" in Munich when asking for information about German translations and performances of *Juno and the Paycock.*

9 Sean O'Casey, *Stücke 1920-1940,* ed. Wolfgang Schuch (East-Berlin: Henschelverlag, 1977). See Manfred Pauli, p. 318.

10 Sean O'Casey, *Rote Rosen für mich. Dramen,* ed. Otto Brandstädter. Translated by Irmhild and Otto Brandstädter (East-Berlin and Weimar: Aufbau-Verlag, 1-66).

11 Sean O'Casey, *Rebell zum Schein. Ausgewählte Stücke.* Translated by Irmhild and Otto Brandstädter (Zürich: Diogenes Verlag, 1966). Sean O'Casey, *Rote Rosen für mich. Dramen.* Translated by Irmhild and Otto Brandstädter, Bibliothek der Weltliteratur (East-Berlin and Weimar: Aufbau-Verlag, 1976).

12 Sean O'Casey, *Dubliner Trilologie: Der Schatten eines Rebellen. Juno und der Pfau. Der Pflug und die Sterne.* Diogenes Taschenbuch 2/II (Zürich: Diogenes Verlag, 1972).

13 Max Beerbohm, "Advice of Those about to Translate Plays", *The Saturday Review of Politics, Literature, Science and Art,* 18 July, 1903, XLVI (London, 1903), p. 76.

14 In Ronald Ayling (ed.), *Blasts and Benedictions: Articles and Stories,* (New York: Macmillan, 1967), pp. 80-81.

15 Sean O'Casey, *Three Plays: Juno and the Paycock. The Shadow of a Gunman. The Plough and the Stars.* Papermac 85 (repr. London: Macmillan, 1972), pp. 5, 8, 25.

16 *Ibid.*, p. 71.

17 Katharine Worth, "O'Casey's Dramatic Symbolism", *Sean O'Casey: Modern Judgements,* ed. Ronald Ayling (London: Macmillan, 1969), pp. 183-184.

CHAPTER 10.

18 Jules Koslow, *Sean O'Casey: The Man and His Plays* (rev. ed., New York, 1966), p. 19.

19 In R. Ayling, pp. 20-26.

20 Sean O'Casey, *Three Plays*, p. 5.

21 Ibid., pp. 8-9.

22 Ibid., p.9.

23 Ibid., pp. 20-21.

24 Ibid., p. 6.

25 Ibid., p. 27.

26 Saros Cowasjee, *Sean O'Casey: The Man behind the Plays* (Edinburgh and London: Oliver and Boyd, 1965), pp. 43-44.

27 Ibid., pp. 45-46.

28 Robert Hogan, *The Experiments of Sean O'Casey* (New York: St. Martin's Press, 1960), P. 152. - See also Thomas Metscher, *Sean O'Caseys dramatischer Stil*. Archiv für das Studium der Neueren Sprachen und Literaturen (Braunschweig, 1968).

29 H.H. Liebrecht, "O'Casey-Aufführungen: Aktuelles Interview mit Eileen O'Casey," *Theater der Zeit*, 11 (1966), p. 3.

30 Ekkerhard Pluta, "Was war: Berlin: O'Caseys 'Juno und der Pfau'", *Theater Heute, XVI*, 2 (1975), p. 54.

31 See the following statements: Paul G. Buchloh and Walter T. Rix, "Wilson John Haires *The Bloom of the Diamond Stone*", in Wilson John Haire, *Los der Hoffnung. Stück in Zwei Akten.* Translated by Paul G. Buchloh and Walter T. Rix (Wien and München: Thomas Sessler, 1976), pp. 1-13. English version: Wilson John Haire, *The Bloom of the Diamond Stone* (London: Pluto Press, 1979).

32 See Paul G. Buchloh and Walter T. Rix. "Wilson John Haire: *Within Two Shadows* und *The Bloom of the Diamond Stone*", *Englische Literatur der Gegenwart 1971-1975*, ed. Rainer Lengeler (Düsseldorf: Bagel Verlag, 1978), pp. 117-131.

CHAPTER 11. TRANSLATION: CHANGING THE CODE: SOYINKA'S IRONIC AETIOLOGY.

1 Henri Meschonnic, *Pour la Poétique* (Paris: Gallimard, 1973) p. 354.

CHAPTER 11.

2 Wole Soyinka, *The Bacchae of Euripides* (London: Eyre Methuen, 1973), p. -i.

All future quotations from this particular book will be identified in the text by inclusion of the page reference in brackets.

3 Geoffrey Stephen Kirk, *The Bacchae by Euripides* (Englewood Cliffs: Prentice Hall, 1970), p. 35.

4 Eric Robertson Dodds, *Euripides Bacchae* (Oxford: Clarendon Press, 1960), pp. xxiii.

4 Kirk, pp. 26-27.

6 Rowland Smith (ed.), *Exile and Tradition* (London: Logman, 1976), p. 69.

7 Kirk, p. 134.

8 Ibid., p. 134.

9 Dodds, pp. 127-128.

10 In Karen L. Morell (ed.), *In Person* (Seattle: University of Washington Press, 1975), pp. 68-69.

11 Wole Soyinka, *Myth, Literature and the African World* (Cambridge, Engl.: Cambridge University Press, 1976), p. 141.

12 Dodds, p. 91.

13 Ibid., p. xii.

14 Ibid., p. xvi.

15 In Morell, p. 117.

16 Hildebrecht Hommel (ed.), *Wege zu Aischylos* (Darmstadt: Wissenschaftliche Buchgesellschaft, 1974), pp. 118-119.

17 Eldred Durosimi Jones, *African Literature Today*, 8 (London: Heinemann, 1976), p. 35.

18 Dodds, p. 172.

19 Ibid., p. 62.

20 Kirk, p. 114.

21 Arthur Sanders Way, *Euripides III* (London: Heinemann and Cambridge, Mass.: Harvard University Press - the Loeb Classical Library, 1950).

CHAPTER 12. THE SYNCHRONIC SALOME.

1 Lines 64-64, "The Daughters of Herodias," *Images of Good and Evil* (1899) *Poems by Arthur Symons*, II (London: William Heinemann, 1911).

2 Cf. Helen Grace Zagona, *The Legend of Salome* (Genève: Droz, 1960).

3 Jacob Grimm, *Teutonic Mythology*, 4th ed., trans. by James Steven Stallybrass (London: George Bell, 1882-1883). Grimm is probably Heine's chief non-authobiographical source for his Herodias in *Atta Troll* (1841).

4 I am not satisfied with Mario Praz' generally accepted explanation that *Atta Troll* brought Herodias/Salome into French literature (cf. *The Romantic Agony*, trans. Angus Davidson (London: Oxford, second ed., 1970), p. 313). The motifs, as I have demonstrated elsewhere, are essentially dissimilar (cf. "Always a man's head falls because of them," Humanities Research Centre, Australian National University, June 30, 1977).

5 (Paris: Charpentier et Fasquelle, 1892), pp. 77-78.

6 *A Study of Oscar Wilde* (London: Charles J. Sawyer, 1930), pp.24, 57.

7 Stanley Weintraub, *Beardsley* (New York: George Braziller, 1967), p. 59. Beardsley's illustrations of *Salome* are among his best known, and Symons put a lugubrious check on the ricochet by writing eight poems "Studies in Strange Sins: After Beardsley's Designs" on these illustrations.

8 "Considérations sur l'art du ballet et la Loïe Fuller," *National Observer* (March 13, 1893).

9 Mallarmé worked on his dramatic fragment for thirty years.

10 Wilde had help with the French from Stuart Merrill, Alfred Retté, André Gide, Marcel Schwob, and Pierre Louÿs. He massively revised Lord Alfred Douglas' English translation. V. Philippe Jullian, *Oscar Wilde*, trans. Violet Wyndham (New York: Viking, 1969), p. 246; Christopher S. Nassar, *Into the Demon Universe* (Yale University Press, 1974), pp. 80-81.

11 Within a decade it was translated also into Catalan, Czech, Dutch, Greek, Italian, Hungarian, Russian, Polish, Spanish, Swedish, and Yiddish.

12 "Entropy and Redundancy in Decadent Style," *Sub-stance*, no. 16 (1977), 144-48; "Translating the Decadent Idiom," *Equivalences*, 6e année (1976), 1-7.

CHAPTER 12.

13 For example, their adaptations of Phèdre's declaration: Lowell *Racine's Phaedra* (London: Faber and Faber, 1963), pp. 42-43; Harrison, *Phaedra Britannica* (London: Rex Collings, 1975), pp. 22-24.

14 "Poetry and Drama" (1950) in Richard Levin, *Tragedy* (New York: Harcourt Brace and World, 1965), p. 143.

15 (Paris: Editions G. Crès, 1925), pp. 76-77; (Berlin: Globus Verlag, n.d.), p. 52; *Plays* (Baltimore: Penguin, 1940), p. 346. Richard Howard, who recently translated Wilde's French into neutral American idiom, renders these lines "Tell the soldiers to go down there and bring me what I want, what the Tetrarch promised me, what belongs to me" (*Shenandoah, XXIX*, Summer, 1978, p. 36). Since Howard's translation has a much shorter syllable count, it would not be singable.

16 Walter Panofsky, *Richard Strauss* (München: R. Piper, 1965), pp. 111, 122-23; Norman del Mar, *Richard Strauss*, I (Philadelphia: Chilton Book Co., 1962), pp. 239ff. When Strauss made the French transcription for the Opera production, May 5, 1907, he meticulously followed the advice of Romain Rolland; *Richard Strauss and Romain Rolland Correspondence* (University of California Press, 1968), pp. 53-77.

17 Del Mar, p. 270

18 Ibid., p. 274.

19 G. Schirmer Libretto (New York, 1964), p. 14.

The writer wishes to express her appreciation to the Center for Modern Theater Research (formerly the Max Reinhardt Archives) of the State University of New York at Binghamton and to the Humanities Research Centre of the Australian National University.

CHAPTER 13. TRANSLATING LITERATURE/TRANSLATED LITERATURE: THE STATE OF THE ART.

1 On the vagaries of the term "equivalence", see:

Bouton, L.F., 1976. "The Problem of Equivalence in Contrastive Analysis", *IRAL*, 14: 143-163.

Catford, J.C., 1965. *A Linguistic Theory of Translation* (London: Oxford University Press)

Durisin, D., 1972. "Die Aequivalenz in der literarischen und nichtliterarischen Übersetzung", *Slavica Slovaca*, 7: 354-377.

CHAPTER 13.

1 cont. Holmes, J.S., 1974. "On Matching and Making Maps", *Delta*, 16 (nr. 4): 67-82.

Jäger, G., 1968. "Elemente einer Theorie der bilingualen Translation", *Grundfragen der Übersetzungswissenschaft. (Beihefte zur Zeitschrift Fremdsprachen)* II: 35-52. Leipzig.

Koller, W., 1972. *Grundprobleme der Übersetzungstheorie* (Bern & München: Fink).

Kuepper, J.J., 1977. "Literary Translation and the Problem of Equivalency", *Meta*, 22: 243-251.

Neubert, A. 1970. "Elemente einer allgemeinen Theorie der Translation", *Actes du Xe Congrès International des Linguistes*, 1967, Bucarest, II: 451-456.

Neubert, A. & O. Kade, eds., 1973. *Neue Beiträge zu Fragen der Übersetzungswissenschaft* (Frankfurt: Athenäum).

Nida, E.A., 1964. *Toward a Science of Translating* (Leiden: Brill).

Popovič, A., 1972. "Die Stellung der Übersetzungstheorie im System der Literaturwissenschaft", *Slavica Slovaca*, 7: 378-395.

Schwarze, C., 1975. "Empirische Probleme des Sprachvergleichs", *Linguistische Berichte*, 35: 10-24.

Tarnoczi, L., 1967. "Congruence entre l'Original et la Traduction", *Babel*, 13: 137-143.

Van den Broeck, R., 1978. "The Concept of Equivalence in Translation Theory: Some Critical Reflections", in J.S. Holmes et al., eds. *Literature and Translation* (Leuven: Acco) 29-47.

Wills, W., 1977. *Übersetzungswissenschaft* (Stuttgart: Klett).

Zemb, J.M., 1972. "Le même et l'autre: Les deux sources de la traduction" *Langages*, 7 (nr 28): 85-101.

2 On the concept of "text" as applicable to translation studies see:

Bühler, K., 1934. *Sprachtheorie* (Jena).

Drescher, W. & S. Scheffzek, eds., 1976. *Theorie und Praxis des Übersetzens und Dolmetschens* (Bern & Frankfurt: Lang).

CHAPTER 13.

2 cont. Gülich, E. & W. Raible, eds., 1977. *Linguistische Textmodelle. Grundlagen und Möglichkeiten* (München: Fink)

Halliday, M.A.K. & R. Hasan, 1977. *Cohesion in English* (London: Longman).

Irmen, F., 1971. "Das Problem der Textarten in übersetzungsrelevanter Sicht" in G. Nickel, ed., *IRAL Sonderband: Kongressbericht der 2. Jahrestagung der Gesellschaft für angewandte Linguistik*, 49-55 (Heidelberg: Groos).

Jakobson, R., 1960. "Linguistics and Poetics" in T.A. Sebeok, ed., *Style in Language*, 350-377 (Cambridge, Mass.: MIT).

Kapp, V., ed., 1974. *Übersetzer und Dolmetscher* (Heidelberg: Quelle).

Reiss, K., 1971. *Möglichkeiten und Grenzen der Übersetzungskritik* (München: Hueber).

Reiss, K., 1975. "Das Problem der Textklassifikation in angewandt-linguistischer Sicht", *Linguistica Antverpiensia*, 9: 43-60.

Reiss, K., 1976. *Texttyp und Übersetzungsmethode* (Kronberg: Scriptor).

Werlich, E., 1975. *Typologie der Texte* (Heidelberg: Quelle & Meyer).

Wills, W. & G. Thome, eds., 1974. *Aspekte der theoretischen sprachenpaarbezogenen und angewandten Übersetzungswissenschaft* (Heidelberg: Groos).

3 There are many linguistic models of the translation process.

A. Syntactic models can be found in:

Tosh, W., 1965. *Syntactic Translation* (The Hague: Mouton).

Yngve, V.H., 1957. "A Framework for Syntactic Translation", *Mechanical Translation*, 4: 59-65.

B. Transformational models are given in:

Nida, E.A., 1964. *Toward a Science of Translating* (Leiden:Brill)

Nida, E.A., 1969. "Science of Translation", *Language*, 45: 483-498.

CHAPTER 13.

3 cont. Nida, E.A. & C.R. Taber, 1969. *The Theory and Practice of Translation* (Leiden: Brill).

Vasiliu, E., 1972. *Outline of a Semantic Theory of Kernel Sentences* (The Hague: Mouton).

Walmsley, J.B., 1970. "Transformation Theory and Translation", *IRAL*, 8 (nr 3): 185-199.

C. A generative model is supplied by:

Levy, J., 1967. "Translation as a Decision Process" in *To Honor Roman Jakobson*, vol. 3: 1171-1182 (The Hague: Mouton).

D. An integrated model has been proposed in:

Holmes, J.S., J. Lambert & R. Van den Broeck, eds., 1978. *Literature and Translation* (Leuven: Acco).

E. Finally, models based on information theory can be found in:

Jäger, G., 1975. *Translation and Translationslinguistik* (Halle: Niemeyer).

Ljudskanov, A., 1975. *Mensch und Maschine als Übersetzer* (Halle: Niemeyer).

4 On the evolution of translational norms, see:

Brower, R.A., 1959. "Seven Agamemnons" in R.A. Brower, ed., *On Translation* 173-195 (New York: OUP).

Bruce, F.F., 1970. *The English Bible: A History of Translation* (London: Lutterworth).

Huber, T., 1968. *Studien zur Theorie des Übersetzens im Zeitalter der deutschen Aufklärung* (Meisenheim am Glan: Anton Hain).

Huysen, A. 1969. *Die frühromantische Konzeption von Übersetzung und Aneignung* (Zürich: Atlantis).

Kahn, L.W., 1935. *Shakespeares Sonette in Deutschland* (Bern: Gotthelf).

Kloepfer, R., 1967. *Die Theorie der literarischen Übersetzung* (München: Fink)

Lefevere, A., 1975. *Translating Poetry: Seven Strategies and a Blueprint* (Assen: Van Gorcum)

CHAPTER 13.

4 cont. Lefevere, A., 1977. *Translating Literature: The German Tradition* (Assen: Van Gorcum).

Mounin, G., 1955. *Les Belles Infidèles* (Paris: Gallimard).

Sdun, W., 1967. *Probleme und Theorien des Übersetzens in Deutschland vom 18. bis zum 20. Jahrhundert* (München: Hueber).

Steiner, T.R., 1975. *English Translation Theory 1650-1800* (Assen: Van Gorcum).

5 The problem of norms is treated systematically in:

Holmes, J.S., 1972. "Rebuilding the Bridge at Bommel: Notes on the Limits of Translatability", *Dutch Quarterly Review*, 2: 65-72.

Popovič, A., 1967. "Die theoretischen Probleme der Übersetzung", *Literatur und Kritik*, 20: 611-627.

Toury, G., 1978. "The Nature and Role of Norms in Literary Translation" in J.S. Holmes, et al., eds., *Literature and Translation*, 83-100 (Leuven: Acco).

Toury, G., 1979. *Norms of Literary Translation into Hebrew* (Tel Aviv: The Porter Institute for Poetics and Semiotics).

6 Relatively recent linguistic definitions of translation are given in:

Catford, J.C., 1965. *A Linguistic Theory of Translation* (London: OUP)

Gachechiladze, G.R., 1967. "Realism and Dialectics in the Art of Translation", *Babel*, 13: 87-91.

Jakobson, R., 1959. "On Linguistic Aspects of Translation" in Brower, R.A. ed., *On Translation*, 232-239 (New York: OUP)

Neubert, A., 1970. "Elemente einer allgemeinen Theorie der Translation" in *Actes du Xe Congres International des Linguistes 1967 Bucarest*, II: 451-456.

Nida, E.A., 1964. *Toward a Science of Translating* (Leiden: Brill).

Oettinger, A.G., 1960. *Automatic Language Translation* (Cambridge, Mass.: Harvard University Press).

Scheibe, E., 1963. "Zum Problem der maschinellen Übersetzung von Sprachen" in *Die Kunst der Übersetzung*, 186-205 (München: Oldenbourg).

CHAPTER 13.

7 "Depressingly normative" or highly speculative theories of translations formulated on the basis of literary criteria are to be found in:

Adams, R.M., 1973. *Proteus, His Lies, His Truth* (New York: Norton).

Brower, R.A., ed., 1959. *On Translation* (New York: OUP)

Gadamer, H.G., 1960. *Wahrheit und Methode* (Tübingen: Mohr).

Heidegger, M., 1958. *Der Satz vom Grund* (Pfüllingen: Neske).

Italiaander, R., ed., 1965. *Übersetzen* (Frankfurt: Athenäum).

Proetz, V., 1971. *The Astonishment of Words* (Austin & London: University of Texas Press).

Raffel, B., 1971. *The Forked Tongue* (The Hague: Mouton).

Savory, T., 1968. *The Art of Translation* (London: Cape).

Steiner, G., 1975. *After Babel* (London: Oxford University Press).

1970. *The World of Translation* (New York: PEN).

8 On the polysystem theory as it is being elaborated and its relationship with translation theory see:

Even Zohar, I., 1978. *Papers in Historical Poetics* (Tel Aviv: The Porter Institute for Poetics and Semiotics).

Even Zohar, I., 1979. "Polysystem Theory", *Poetics Today*, 1, 1-2: 287-310.

Lefevere, A., 1977. *Literary Knowledge* (Assen: Van Gorcum)

Lefevere, A., 1978. "Towards a Science of Literature", *Dispositio*, 3, 7-8: 71-84.

Lefevere, A., 1978. "Some Tactical Steps toward a Common Poetics", *New Asia Academic Bulletin*, 1: 9-16.

Lefevere, A. & Van den Broeck, R., 1980. *An Invitation to a Science of Translation* (Assen: Van Gorcum).

Toury, G. & I. Even Zohar, eds., 1979. *Proceedings of the Colloquium on Translation and Intercultural Relations, Tel Aviv 1978.* (Tel Aviv: The Porter Institute for Poetics and Semiotics).

CHAPTER 13.

9 Although many monographs of X as translator of Y exist in the field of drama translation, none, to my knowledge, go beyond treating drama as simply the text on the page. There is, therefore, practically no theoretical literature on the translation of drama as acted and produced. It is hoped that the present volume may help direct the attention of scholars to this virtually virgin field of research.